UNDER GROTTO MOUNTAIN
RAT'S NEST CAVE

D0746112

Charles J. Yonge

Rocky
Mountain Books

Mineral formations in the Great West Highway. Flowstone muddied by careless cavers. Photo Dixon Thompson.

UNDER GROTTO MOUNTAIN
RAT'S NEST CAVE

Charles J. Yonge

Rocky
Mountain Books

Front cover: The author in Ranger Way. Photo Ian Drummond.
Back cover: Phil Riel negotiating the Laundry Chute. Photo Matt Riel.

Photographs provided by the author unless otherwise credited.

We acknowledge the financial support of the Government of Canada through the Book Publishing Industry Development Program (BPIDP) for our publishing activities.

Printed and bound in Canada by AGMY Marquis Imprimeur Inc.

Copyright © 2001 Charles Yonge
Second printing 2006

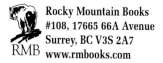

Rocky Mountain Books
#108, 17665 66A Avenue
Surrey, BC V3S 2A7
RMB www.rmbooks.com

ISBN 0-921102-77-1

National Library of Canada Cataloguing in Publication Data

Yonge, Charles J.
  Under Grotto Mountain

Includes index.
ISBN 0-921102-77-1

  1. Grotto Mountain (Alta.)--Guidebooks. 2. Caves--Alberta--Grotto Mountain--
    Guidebooks. I. Title.
GV200.66.C32G76 2001   917.123'32   C2001-910018-3

Contents

Foldout cave map in pocket at end of book

Acknowledgements

The concept of writing about Rat's Nest Cave began around 12 years ago, soon after it became a Provincial Historic Site. Following a number of reports and published papers *Under Grotto Mountain* has finally emerged.

I would therefore like to thank the Alberta Historic Resources Foundation and the Alberta Environmental Trust for financial support at the research stage in the form of generous grants. Dr. H. Roy Krouse, past director of the Stable Isotope Laboratory (now professor emeritus) at the University of Calgary and Dr. Derek C. Ford, professor emeritus in the Department of Geography and Geology at McMaster University for providing their laboratory services for the dating and climate work. Dr. Krouse also supported me as a research associate at that time. I am very grateful also for support down the years from Mr. Barry Newton of the Historic Resources Division, Alberta Community Development, and Dr. James Burns from the Provincial Museum of Alberta, the latter who freely offered his palaeontological findings for publication here.

A huge amount of volunteer support over the years has come from members of the Alberta Speleological Society, and rather than naming them individually, I urge you to look in the index where reference to their assistance may be found. However, a few names here are in order: Dave Thomson for photographs and as an indispensable research assistant, Ian McKenzie for photographs and much support in committees, meetings and as editor of the *Journal of Subterranean Metaphysics* (the ASS Newsletter), Ian Drummond for some excellent photographs including the cover, and for cave radio assistance with the survey, Jon Rollins, who managed our project with the *Science Alberta Foundation,* from which our cave tours were born, and for concern over management issues at the cave and finally David Brandreth, through his company, Clarion Geophysical, for getting the cave map into electronic form.

A number of individuals critiqued and generally improved various chapters in the book. Pam Henson and Cheryl Wilcocks (English teachers), Pam Yonge and Peter Zabrok got after me for bad grammar and turgid prose; they unravelled numerous convoluted sentences and rewrote them in plain English. Jon Donovan, with prompts from Pete Thompson and Ian Drummond helped enormously to get the historical record of cave exploration straight. Dave Lowe of the British Geological Survey and Ben Gadd of the Jasper Institute, both geologists, were of great assistance in the geology sections—for accuracy, suggestions and again for good English. Dr. James Burns of the Provincial Museum of Alberta red-penned my cave life chapter, and made sure I knew when and when not to use italics in the formal tabulation of species.

Finally, I must thank the Alberta Arts Foundation who had enough faith in my application to award me the project Writers' Individual #99/8740. Their grant got me started, got me committed, and I think it is fair to say this book probably wouldn't have happened without them.

Preface

This book is about one cave, Rat's Nest Cave. The cave is one of the myriad of limestone caves found across our planet, and like many of those others it has an interesting story to tell. Every cave is unique.

The cave lies under the forested flanks of Grotto Mountain close to the town of Canmore in the Bow Valley. Few caves have been found in the "Bow Corridor," probably because their entrances are obscured by glacial sediments, scree or some such feature, rather than the lack of the right cave forming rock—limestone. The cave is adjacent to Banff National Park, which sees more than four million visitors a year. The growing resort town of Canmore is only 5 km to the west and the cave is within driving distance of Calgary, a city whose population will probably exceed one million in the next decade. Therefore the cave, nestled as it is in a wild canyon close to civilization—seemingly a wilderness setting—is of growing interest to visitors who seek the mountainous splendour of our area.

Caves have held a fascination for humankind down the ages and Rat's Nest Cave is no exception. It seems people have visited the cave for more than 3000 years, then as now, the cave has been the focus of their interest. While 3000 years ago the cave may have provided a hunting retreat and a place for spiritual meditation, the adventurous challenge offered by three-dimensional passageways and the natural history of its varied features are the attractions today.

While the cave offers an adventure experience that is physically rigorous, in this book I want to emphasize its natural history, its *speleology*, as well as the rich exploration experiences documented. Speleology is one of the newest sciences and it has expanded incredibly over the last few decades. Many university and government departments embrace aspects of it, consultants find work in the field and numerous international conferences are held worldwide. Cave and cave landscapes provide a wide variety of recreational pleasures, for often the finest scenery can be found in such regions. Rat's Nest Cave and its environs are in many ways a microcosm of all of these aspects and I present the book to you in this vein.

Further Reading

Ford, D. C. F. and Williams, P., 1989. *Karst Geomorphology and Hydrology*. London: Unwin Hyman, 601 pp.

Ford, D. C. F. and Muir, D., 1985. *Castleguard*. Parks Canada Centennial Edition.

Gadd, B., 1995. *Handbook of the Canadian Rockies (2nd edition)*. Jasper, Alberta: Corax Press, 831 pp.

Gillieson, D. S., 1996. *Caves: Processes, Development and Management*. Oxford: Blackwell, 324 pp.

Hill, C. A. and Forti, P., 1984. *Cave Minerals of the World*. National Speleological Society Press, 238 pp.

Huck, B. and Whiteway, D., 1998. *In Search of Ancient Alberta*. Winnipeg, Manitoba: Heartland Publications, 287 pp.

Moore, G. W. and Sullivan, G. N., 1964. *Speleology: The Study of Caves*. Zephyrus Press Inc., 150 pp.

Parfit, M. December 2000. Dawn of Humans: Hunt for the first Americans. *National Geographic*, 40-67 pp.

Pybus, M., 1988. *Bats of Alberta*. Edmonton, Alberta: Alberta Forestry, Lands and Wildlife.

Rollins, J., 1999. *Rat's Nest Cave Management Report*. Edmonton, Alberta: Unpublished Report for Alberta Provincial Historic Resources.

Rollins, J. L., 1992. *Caves of the Canadian Rockies*. University of Calgary: Unpublished Master's Defence Project, 1992.

Thompson, P., 1976. *Cave Exploration in Canada*. Stalactite Press, 183 pp.

Yonge, C. J., 1991. Studies at Rat's Nest Cave: Potential for an Underground Laboratory in the Canadian Rocky Mountains. *BCRA. Cave and Karst Science*, Vol. 18, No. 3, 119-129 pp.

Yonge, C. J., 1990. *Rat's Nest Cave*. Edmonton, Alberta: Unpublished Report for Alberta Provincial Historic Resources.

How the book is organized

Chapter 1 takes you on a tour of the cave—a tour currently you can do with qualified guides. On the tour there are a number of interpretive stops, which are described briefly. But should any of the "interpretive moments" grab your interest, you can dive into a later chapter to read about it in more detail.

For example, you pause to observe a bushy-tailed wood rat comfortably curled up in its midden, or in the corner of your eye a bat flits by, or a bone fragment on the floor catches your attention. All of this can be read about in Chapter 8 *Cave Life and the Bone Bed.* As you crawl flat out down a rock tube for several body lengths trying to keep panic from surfacing, you might ponder the explorers who were doing this for the first time. They didn't have the benefit of knowing where this passage went or a guide to reassure them. Well, turn to Chapter 11 and read *Modern Exploration.*

You may be interested in cave science. How did the cave form? How old is it? How do you turn back the clock and determine its *paleoenvironment?* There are a few chapters on geological and geomorphological aspects, which put the cave into perspective—it's old, it was intimately associated with the numerous Rocky Mountain glaciations and so on. Chapters 4, 5 and 6 give you that sequential story.

Rat's Nest Cave is a Provincial Historic Site and is therefore an Albertan heritage. Cave sites need appropriate management strategies, as they are limited, fragile spaces. As the population of Calgary approaches one million and tourism in the Bow Valley continues to grow apace, the cave will need a good and sensible protection approach for its posterity. Chapter 12 addresses management issues and the cave's future.

Speleology, as with other sciences, has an arcane language. I have therefore included a glossary to assist the reader who is not a speleologist to wade through the more technical sections.

I trust the reader will find some corner of interest here.

Charles J. Yonge, February 2001

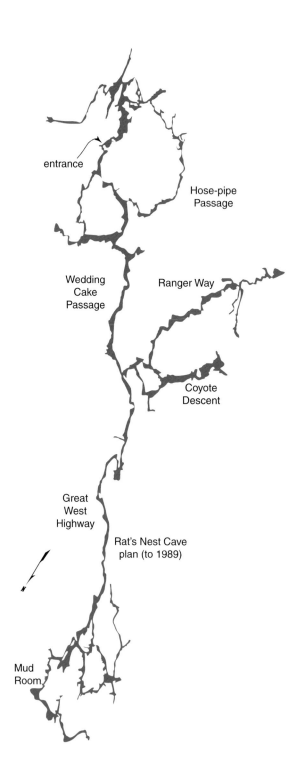

entrance

Hose-pipe
Passage

Wedding
Cake
Passage

Ranger Way

Coyote
Descent

Great
West
Highway

Rat's Nest Cave
plan (to 1989)

N

Mud
Room

I Touring Rat's Nest Cave

While Rat's Nest Cave is a physically demanding place and offers high adventure, it is also a museum of time transporting you back through 300 million years of natural history and 3000 years of human history. It's because of this fascinating history that the cave has been designated a Provincial Historic Site by the government of Alberta. In the chapters ahead you will find a detailed account of the interpretation that is offered by experienced cave guides, and also of how the interpretive material was researched and developed. My company, Canmore Caverns Limited, currently runs guided trips into the cave and has been doing so for the last eight years or so. Here we follow one of our tours.

It is early summer and the day dawns cool with a subtle hint of rain in the air. That's not too serious, as we will be spending most of our time underground, probably about three hours or so. The cave is cool and fairly dry, conditions that do not vary much year round. My group today represents the more adventurous cross-section of visitors to the mountain parks. The German couple has camped at Two Jack Lake in Banff National Park—they work as computer specialists in Hamburg and are on vacation (in fact, they booked us from Germany earlier in the year through our web site). The Japanese student is employed at the International Hotel in Banff and this is her day off. She is doing a degree in tourism at the University of Osaka. The North American family is taking advantage of the cheap Canadian dollar and avoiding the heat of summertime U.S. They are teachers from New York state with their teenage daughter in high school. Finally, I have a honeymooning couple from Manitoba, who work in financial services. Besides the German couple who are camping, everyone is staying in hotels, reflecting a change from a few years ago when most hotel-based visitors did little more than shop and look at mountain views from rented cars. Now a high proportion of visitors looks for a physically challenging as well as informative experience.

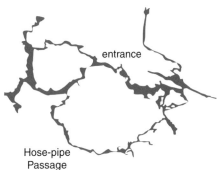

Diagram of the tour section of the caves.

Grotto Mountain seen across the Bow Valley. Canmore is in the middle distance. Note the limestone quarry scar on the right side of the mountain. The cave lies in a valley on the right skyline. Photo Dave Thomson.

We park in a gravel quarry directly below a small valley where the cave will be found. The area is zoned as industrial and the cave entrance is on the lease of Graymont Western Canada Inc., from whom we must seek permission to enter the cave as they are the site custodians. Our hike to the cave climbs steeply out of the quarry and up onto a level area consisting of glacial alluvial deposits (referred to as benches). The mountain views are excellent here so we stop for a breather. These benches are grass-covered and are swept clear of snow by strong westerly winds during the winter when it is a good time to see bighorn sheep that like to graze there. It is presently carpeted with wildflowers and dotted about are eye-catching tiger lilies and Indian paintbrush forming a sea of red and orange. Looking across the great glacial U-shaped Bow Valley we can see one of the highest mountains in the area, Mount Lougheed at 3107 m, and the forest-filled Wind Valley below it. The recently proposed urban development of Wind Valley has been contentious and the subject of public debates. In fact, as we look down the Bow Valley corridor toward Canmore, we see human growth usurping the precious montane ecosystem on the valley floor. How will this view look to our grandchildren?

Nevertheless the views are truly breathtaking. We are in a sense looking at a vast slice of geological time. The impending limestone faces on the surrounding mountains date back to ancient ocean environments in the Devonian and Lower Carboniferous beginning some 410 million years ago. The Lower Carboniferous limestone is also the rock that our cave is formed in. The valley is floored by dinosaur-aged coal measures on which Canmore is built and that shaped its economy over 100 years ago. Finally, the U-shaped Bow Valley, repeatedly gouged by advancing glaciers until 13,000 years ago, marks the last major geological event. The bench we stand on is made up of deposits left by those glaciers. How does the cave fit into this geological history? We shall see.

We pick up the cave valley from the bench we are on, and hike beside the creekbed through lodgepole evergreen forest, which mantles the lower slopes of Grotto Mountain. Squirrels are abundant, chirping with bird-like calls. The creek is dry and runs rarely—although since the recent year of El Nino, this has actually proved to be an exception. The trail is pleasant and maintains an easy grade, until closing valley walls force us into a canyon. The canyon gives a sense of wilderness, as it contains no trail necessitating a couple of short scrambles before reaching the cave.

Among other trees, Rocky Mountain maple grows in the canyon, which indicates a very sheltered spot. This maple is rare in Alberta, but here it provides an important food source for the bushy-tailed wood rats living in the cave. Eventually we drop our packs opposite the cave entrance, which is seen as a wide, low-arched opening up a short slope in the base of the canyon wall. It's intriguing that 4 km of cave lies behind this entrance. While changing into our caving gear, one of the visitors comments that all the equipment reminds them of getting ready for a scuba dive. There is a lot of equipment, but this is not a stroll. We really are going caving. So we don climbing harnesses, coveralls (there's mud!), helmet, battery pack, headlamp and gloves and we move into the twilight zone of the entrance where we can still see without lights.

The cave valley on Grotto Mountain. The cave lies in the trees below the sunlit outcrop. Photo Dave Thomson.

A caver in the canyon on the way to the cave in winter.

For some visitors this is a nerve-wracking time as the contrast between "out" and "in" is very marked and they have now crossed that threshold. Beyond lies darkness and mystery, a very unfamiliar world to most. "Can I cope with this?" may well be a silent question on their minds. The guide's reassurance is important, but so too is the introduction. Entrances are often one of the most interesting features of a cave, a transition from light to dark where a lot of things go on, perhaps somewhat analogous to the seashore.

The entrance takes the form of an alcove with a 15 m-deep pit in its rock floor. For more than 7000 years animals and debris have fallen into this pit. The skeletal remains of 34 different mammal species have been found at its base along with prehistoric Indian stone implements. The cave has had visitors for more than 3000 years! Ledges above the pit are strewn with nesting material where bushy-tailed wood rats (or pack rats) have not only stored maple and other vegetation for winter feed, but also plastic, fleece and other human detritus. Pack rats do a good job of picking up after careless humans. Stacks of mushrooms in the nests intrigue me—a vet on a previous trip told me the MSG in mushrooms is a good source of nourishment. One of my German guests tells me it's for "hallucinogenic entertainment" during the boring winter months when other sensible creatures hibernate. The ceiling of the alcove is multifaceted, beautifully sculptured into whorls, hollows and flutes. In these are a number of insects and spiders—notably mosquitoes and harvesters (or daddy long-legs). As the cave never freezes, it is an important hibernaculum for them. Very occasionally we see bats on our guided trips—mostly little brown bats. Because of the small number of bat sightings in the cave, we believe

The cave entrance. Photo Dave Thomson.

there may be a well-populated bat hibernaculum yet to be discovered.

Before our tour sets off, I explain we are actually entering a relict spring now abandoned and that at one time all the passageways in the cave were filled with water. In fact, during the several glaciations water must have flowed up the bone pit and thundered out into the canyon. The sloping rock face outside the entrance exhibits such flow marks. I also point out that the entrance may not have always existed and that it appeared as a breach in the cave passage when the canyon was being cut down from outside. Such canyons are very common in the area, having been eroded by dynamic streams entrained under rotting ice

A bushy-tailed wood rat in its nest.
Photo Dave Thomson.

sheets during periods of glacial retreat. We proceed inward from the entrance via a downward passage at one side of the alcove. This is where the water used to flow to prior to breaching of the cave passage, after coming up the pit; the elegant swirls and solution pockets in the ceiling indicate this. There are pack rat nests inside and one obliging creature is curled up in its nest. The negatively emotive term "rat" is hardly fair, they're like large hamsters with bushy tails and really very cute.

The descent is now tricky, especially as our eyes are adjusting to the dark and we try to follow the headlamp's circular beam. If you can cope with this then the rest of trip will not be a problem, I say. Actually, the cave seems bewildering: passages go in every direction and jumbles of boulders are confusing. For those of us unfamiliar with cave environments, the darkness and confusion push our psychological comfort zone. The descent ends in a large boulder-floored chamber. We turn our lights out here and the darkness closes around us completely. Even a hand waved in front of the eyes registers nothing. You are totally blind here, despite being so close to the entrance. Along with the dark, the cave interior experiences almost unchanging conditions. Temperature and humidity remain at 5°C and 100 per cent year round. On very cold days in winter, the relatively warm, moist air steams out of the entrance and freezes as a spectacular rime on the canyon wall. Such conditions in the cave mean we can run guided trips here at any time of the year. The conditions will only change over thousands of years as the climate changes.

The way out of the chamber is not obvious until we perceive a circular hole at head level in the back wall. Hauling ourselves into it, we then squeeze along a diagonal slot ending at a shaft with a rope descending

Grand Gallery. Photo John Gantor.

Moonmilk deposits on the wall above the cav-
er's head. Photo Dave Thomson.

into blackness. This is one of the adventure highlights of the trip for we must rappel 18 m into the cavern below. Only one person in our group, the teenager, has rappelled before—at a camp in the New York Catskill Mountains—so she goes first and has the job of helping the others when they reach the bottom. Meanwhile, I operate a safety line from above in case there is a problem. When the time comes for the others to descend, trepidation turns to "wow I can do this," to exhilaration and wonderment as the features of the shaft unfold. One wall is completely white, covered with a moist chemical or bacterial deposit known as moonmilk. From midway a steeply dipping tube leads off to other routes into the cave, a truly three-dimensional maze.

At the base of the shaft we intersect a large passage leading downward. Boulders litter the floor and the intricate ceiling with its whorls and intestinal-like tubes is high over our heads. One of those tubes is inviting—in fact, earmarked as a climb into new territory and has one of our ropes hanging down it. Yes, the cave is still being explored to this day. Entering now a connecting chamber, we see pack rat bones littering the floor or bones dragged in by pack rats. These are variously ribs, skull fragments, vertebrae, ball and socket joints all chewed to roundness by pack rats who need calcium in their diets. A forking passage takes us on to our (optional) caving testpiece: the psychologically taxing Laundry Chute, an appropriate name adopted by clients during prior struggles there. An impossibly tight looking slot penetrates vertically to a constricted tube that angles downward for several body lengths. Fortunately, we only have to go through this one-way as part of our round trip and of course it can be avoided if the round trip is not done.

My group is fit and they are willing to "take a look." The first person slithers sideways feet-first down the chimney. This is followed by a right-angle bend into the tube, very awkward for tall people, and a backward stomach drag down the constricted channel. To add to the adrenaline flow, this splits into two tight eyeholes at one point. One eye is slightly larger than the other eye—we have a choice! Panic rises, especially when a helmet jams and a light cable catches on jutting rocks, but eventually we slither out via a hand-line into a maze of larger, sloping tunnels. Many of our visitors will have a go at this, and when I ask them to look after the person in front and behind them, the responsibility seems to help conquer some of the anxiety. Nonetheless, we have a good number of visitors understandably not wanting to try the Laundry Chute and we take alternative routes. Just occasionally someone will not even enter the cave, but there is no pressure. Rather, I admire people who are not embarrassed to admit their fear. Many of us are used to being in control of our surroundings on a daily basis; the cave, with its thoroughly unfamiliar and daunting setting, challenges that control.

We've now entered a maze area where the whole cave is tilted at an angle of around 25°. The cave here is well and truly following a thrust fault—a major geological weakness in the bedrock subsequently enlarged by groundwater. In front a minaret-shaped tube descends down the dip of the fault, a beautiful example of where the limestone has been dissolved away along the plane of the fault and along a vertical intersecting joint fracture. This we descend for over 40 m until its end in a moist, sandy choke. Here we are excavating a tiny drafting tube by removing the sandy floor with a small shovel. This so-called dig represents another method of exploration in the cave. A similar dig of ours in another part of the cave led to the discovery of almost 2 km of new passageways, never travelled by humans. Cavers are fascinated by exploration, places where no one's ever been...still much of the underground remains a mystery.

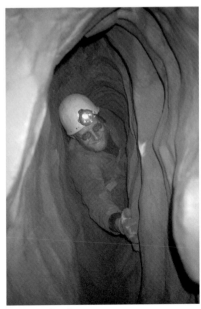

Here we pause for something to eat. It is also a great spot for sensory deprivation. Turning out our lights, we lie back on the sand and experience something one almost

The Laundry Chute.

17

never can outside—darkness and silence in totality. Our ears ring, but it's all coming from within.

Climbing back up the tube is yet another physical challenge. It seems you can almost never hike in this three-dimensional multi-level place, instead you must shimmy, slide, grovel, thrutch (a caver's word) using all parts of your body to get around. I remember an old caving friend who introduced me to the activity, advising me to cave with an "economy of energy." Careful movement, good footwork and stamina are essential facets of the experienced caver. During the upward thrutch we pass a strongly drafting tube at ceiling height not remarked on on the descent. The draft signals a large amount of cave beyond, some 3 km, in fact. However, to get there from this point requires

Descending the second climb from the entrance. Photo Ian Drummond.

you to negotiate the dreaded Hose-pipe Passage, which is equivalent to many Laundry Chutes coupled with a flat-out grovel through water on your back, nose out against the ceiling. A much more pleasant alternative for accessing the back regions of the cave is to descend the bone shaft at the entrance to which this passage joins.

Passing below the Laundry Chute, we follow the maze back the other way, down the so-called Treacherous Slab, a slab that trends downward at a seemingly impossible angle into blackness. Actually, it's not as portentous as the name suggests, our coveralls offer a lot of friction making the descent slower than anticipated. We then follow a crawlway at the end of which we thread ourselves up through a boulder-lined hole into a small chamber. The chamber was beautifully decorated in the early days with calcite mineral

formations, but now these formations are mud-streaked with the passage of people. In fact, regrettably, one massive stalagmite has been broken off at half-height and the top taken from the cave. The remaining 10 cm indicate what was there before and our studies of other formations in the cave suggest that perhaps 50,000 years of growth was ended with the blow of a hammer. Fortunately, Rat's Nest Cave has seen relatively little of

A wood rat skeleton. Photo Dave Thomson. such willful vandalism.

From the chamber we carefully crawl around a column—formed by the meeting of the upward growth of a stalagmite and the downward growth of a stalactite—and then on into easier and larger passageways. Here we can see spoon-shaped depressions in the cave walls formed by flowing water. These are called solution scallops, and tell us something about the ancient water flow through the passage. We soon reach a three-way junction, where, in one direction, we can look through a large opening into the gaping blackness of the Grand Gallery, the largest chamber in the system. We enter this massive chamber that has formed along the intersection of two faults. One of the faults runs as a prominent vertical seam right through the chamber, giving rise to passages at each end. The high ceiling and one

Descending the large passage toward the Grand Gallery. Photo Ian Drummond.

overhanging wall are ornamented with mineral formations, and at the base of this wall a mineralized passage leads down into the Grotto. Before traversing the Grand Gallery and descending to the Grotto, we pause to admire the formations. The overhanging wall, by its very nature has given rise to particular formations called curtains. Water droplets, charged with dissolved mineral (bicarbonate), run down the wall leaving a trace of the mineral (calcite) behind. In time, the trace builds to a thin, translucent curtain or drapery, streaked like bacon as the layers vary in composition. At the end of the curtain, the droplet falls, leaving a cone-shaped stalactite and, where it splatters on the floor, a broader-shaped stalagmite. Elongated, hollow soda straws hang from the ceiling and other places where the surface is horizontal.

We descend now into the Grotto, a chamber decorated almost completely with formations. As there are a number of water sources entering here, the mineral formations result from dripping, flowing, seeping, pooled water. Curtains are evident here along with "frozen" honey-coloured streams and waterfalls called flowstone that cascade over areas where the floor and walls are highly inclined. Rimstone dams, terraced like rice paddies, form from water splashing into pools, depositing calcite dams around the edges. A spectacular cloud of soda straws hangs from the ceiling. These deposits are formed by water flowing down the inside of the tube and as the water droplets fall off the end, trace rings of calcite are deposited on the end.

The Grotto marks the end point of the tour as a large, clear pool halts our progress. To continue requires scuba diving, yet another method by

A sloping fault-aligned passage. Photo Ian Drummond.

which we have extended the reaches of Rat's Nest Cave. In fact, four of these sumps, one following the other, have been dived here. The last, which we haven't been able to penetrate, is at the base of a 15 m-high waterfall at one of the deepest points in the cave, 165 m below the entrance. Such exploration is extremely serious and should only be undertaken by trained cave-divers. Lives are all too frequently lost in this gripping sport.

We stop in the Grotto for some time as there are several features of interest and it's a great place for photographs. A moment of quiet reveals the chattering of several small streams and the mysterious hollow drip-drip as water falls to the floor—uniquely cave sounds. Inevitably, the timelessness of the place leads to questions about the age of the formations. Dating these by radioactive methods has revealed an interesting pattern going back some 750,000 years. We find them to have formed in the periods between the ice ages, of which there have been several. It appears that growth stops during ice advances because the ground freezes up as the supply of mineral-laden water is cut off by permafrost. With our lights off, I place a flashgun against one of the formations and discharge it. A disembodied lurid green glow hangs in the dark, fading quickly away. The flash has excited a phenomenon known as luminescence, which comes from minute quantities of organic acids and/or uranium salts trapped in the speleothem calcite (a speleothem is a cave mineral formation). Believe it or not, the intensity of the luminescence can tell us something about past climates and relates to the sun's power over time—more of that in the chapters to come.

Back in the Grand Gallery, we head up a steep slope following the vertical fault seam in the ceiling. And suddenly the roof shoots up to over 30 m as light beams are lost in the blackness overhead. Distantly the ceiling can barely be made out. Drips flare briefly in the light beams before falling heavily into the floor where they have created rather elegantly fluted pits. A few years ago we climbed up this so-called dome-pit, using artificial climbing aids to surmount the overhanging walls, but despite a beckoning draught we could find no way on at the top. To this day, I believe we have missed some elusive lead into caverns unknown.

Some three hours have passed now, so we return to the 18 m pitch via easy passageways. The flexible cable ladder we fixed for the return looks ominous to tired cavers and there is trepidation. However, I climb up first and then bring everyone up on a good, tight lifeline. My clients emit gasps and grunts as they struggle upward, and excitable calls for a tight line float up the pitch as the last challenge is met. Physical and psychological exhaustion have taken its toll, but not unpleasantly. Then remains the final climb out toward the faint glow of daylight and that special smell of the outside, which welcomes us back to normality. We emerge to a beautiful sunny afternoon and feelings of great personal satisfaction—"I did it, I really did it."

It's downhill now to the cars and the Rose and Crown Pub where we'll pore over the map as we relive our trip, a kind of debriefing, I suppose, but in a decidedly relaxed setting.

A tour group in The Grotto. Photo Ian Drummond.

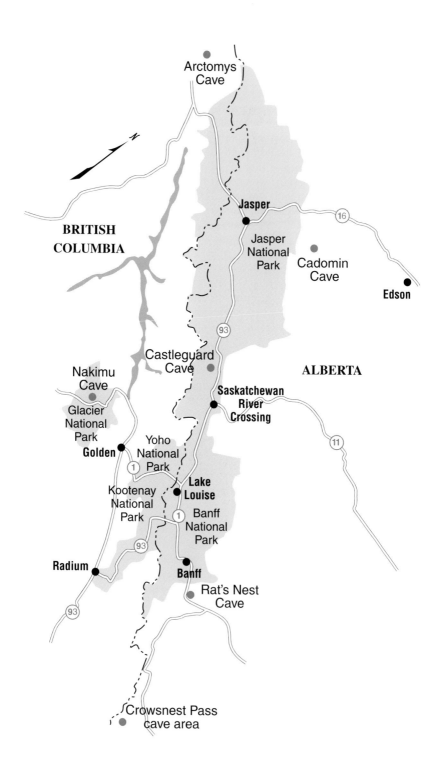

Arctomys
Cave

BRITISH
COLUMBIA

Jasper

Jasper
National
Park

Cadomin
Cave

Edson

16

93

Nakimu
Cave

Castleguard
Cave

ALBERTA

Glacier
National
Park

Saskatchewan
River
Crossing

Golden

Yoho
National
Park

1

Kootenay
National
Park

**Lake
Louise**

11

93

Radium

Banff
National
Park

1

93

Banff

Rat's Nest
Cave

93

Crowsnest Pass
cave area

2 Caving in the Canadian Rockies

Rat's Nest Cave is unique in the Canadian Rocky Mountains for two major reasons: it is a relatively warm cave and is located close to a highway. To get to the entrance you hike less than 2 km, gaining only 180 m in elevation. It is also rather a solid cave unaffected by frost-shattered material, a significant danger when exploring caves in the alpine zone. Caving in the Rockies is marked by long hikes high up into the mountains, often involving overnight camping, with loose, difficult and spectacular caves at the destination.

Serious cave exploration in the Rockies has only come about relatively recently. Prior to 1965 interest in caves was superficial and spasmodic. Mountaineers and naturalists made references to caves in passing but they were seldom explored. A notable exception to this was A. O. Wheeler, who, accompanied by notables from the Alpine Club of Canada—Konrad Kain, Byron Harmon, Donald Phillips and George Kinney—explored 76 m down

The Subway in Castleguard Cave. Photo Russell Harmond.

Icefall Brook. Water pours from a cave entrance in the cliff below the Lyell Icefield.

into Canada's currently deepest cave, Arctomys, in 1911. He also noted several karst spring systems and some other karst features (karst refers to landscapes, which are modified or created by the acid effects of groundwater or falling precipitation—see glossary).

The modern era of cave exploration came with a systematic documentation of Rockies' caves by students and staff at McMaster University under the auspices of Dr. Derek Ford of the geography department. I was, like many others before me, a student of Derek's studying aspects of karst. It was one way of extending one's misspent youth and continuing to cave. About this time too, the Alberta Speleological Society was formed, but there was some rivalry between the groups, a difference in philosophy between the "professionals" at McMaster and the provincial "amateurs." But the ASS made their mark and the club continues strongly to this day. Their (our) newsletter, the *Journal of Subterranean Metaphysics*, suggests a certain irreverent attitude toward the experts.

Caving in the Canadian Rockies requires a good level of fitness and self-reliance. Hikes to and from cave entrances almost invariably require a night or two out. Camping as well as caving equipment must be carried, although occasionally we have used helicopters to access very remote areas. Once in the cave, the trips can be long and potentially dangerous. Very often new ground is being explored because in general the caves are rarely or never visited, which makes the enterprise highly exciting. How often do we, the rank and file, get to tread where no woman or man has ever ventured before?

Castleguard Cave in Banff National Park is Canada's longest with over 20 km of passageways explored. The cave ends in ice-blocked passages right under the Columbia Icefield. Several international expeditions have been attracted to Castleguard Cave. Its position under the Columbia Icefield and its great length necessitating underground camps combined with the harsh winter conditions make it a unique caving experience. Why do we visit the cave in winter? The first explorations were made in the summer, but on one trip two explorers, Pete Thompson and Mike Boon of McMaster University, were trapped behind rising floodwaters for over two days. Eventually short of light and very cold, they were assisted back to daylight by the surface team when the waters subsided. Soon after making the surface, the cave quickly flooded again not only filling the first 600 m of cave to the roof, but the stream rose 8 m up the entrance shaft. So fast did the waters rise that someone sunbathing in the dry stream channel outside the entrance had to scramble to safety. The entrance section then remained flooded for a further 18 days. They were lucky to escape with their lives. Now trips are done in winter or spring and we make our way along those 600 m of flood-prone passage on a river of ice.

Later, Boon made a monumental solo trip (an act of defiance after not being invited on a McMaster University expedition), where he discovered the first of the ice plugs. He had, in fact, ended up right under the Columbia Icefield where ice had intruded the cave. People were skeptical when he returned with his story, but they eventually believed

An undescended shaft in a new cave area, Kootenay National Park.

Exploring a new cave passage in Shorty's Cave, Crowsnest Pass.

Difficult traversing in the Second Fissure, Castleguard Cave. Photo Ian Drummond.

The Ice Plug, Castleguard Cave. Photo Chris Pugsley.

him when they saw an ice plug with their own eyes. I recall being at Boon's Aven several kilometres into the cave and several years later, looking up the 10 m aven at the rusting etriers he had used for his push into the new territory, and reflecting on the sheer audacity of his enterprise. Without doubt this remains one of the more courageous caving trips done in this country.

Although a number of the early trips were supported by helicopter, later trips have been done on skis. (One helicopter actually crashed, becoming a giant rototiller that thrashed its way through the snow. Fortunately the occupants, who included Boon, got clear of it without injury.) To ski in you have to strap on skins and ascend the Saskatchewan Glacier, crossing an avalanche-threatening moraine to gain the Castleguard Meadows. These are descended to the cave at their lower end, a total distance of 17 km.

At the entrance of Fang Cave in the B.C. Rockies. Photo Ian McKenzie.

Exploring the cave is somewhat like climbing a Himalayan peak where staging camps have to be established at intervals along the way. We have spent up to six days in the cave operating from two or even three underground camps in order to explore the far reaches of the cave.

What of deep caves in the Canadian Rockies? Currently, not only is Arctomys Canada's deepest cave, but it is also deeper than any cave in the USA. In fact, you have to go to that caving Mecca, Mexico, before caves of greater depth are found. Far off in Mount Robson Provincial Park it is a 24 km hike to the cave climbing up to an elevation of 2200 m.

In 1971 Mike Goodchild of McMaster and friends descended the cave to find the distinctive footprints of Wheeler and his companions who had ventured here 60 years earlier; tricouni nail marks were still evident. They had stopped where the cave steepened and a waterfall deterred further progress. In a series of trips over the next two years the cave was eventually explored, using wetsuits, to more than half a kilometre in depth (522 m). My companion, Pete Lord and I, while on an early survey trip, vividly recall the Refresher, an 8 m-high waterfall in a narrowing canyon and no way to avoid the full force of the icy water. Fortunately, further roped drops avoid the stream, which cascades through the cave in a series of canyons and falls to a siphon at the bottom. There is a beautifully decorated chamber near the bottom, rather a surprise in that dynamic environment. Incredibly, in an attempt to go deeper, Kirk McGregor of the Toronto Caving Group free-dived the siphon to find a further siphon, which has yet to be penetrated.

Unfortunately, Canadian Rockies' caving has its share of tragedy. In 1991 Rick Black, a stalwart of the Alberta Speleological Society and good friend to all, lost his life after a rockfall a long way into Arctomys Cave. After the

Descending past permanent ice in Serendipity Cave, Crowsnest Pass. Photo Bill MacDonald.

accident, two of the remaining three persons in the party made their way out of the cave to get sleeping bags, while one with first aid training stayed behind. Eventually, fearing that he was suffering from exposure and with Rick's agreement, he left the cave too, emerging after a gruelling 43 hours underground. As it was, the first two could not return to the cave for lack of light and so they made the long trek to the road to get help instead. A huge rescue was mounted involving most of the cavers from western Canada, but it was almost two days before they reached Rick. By this time, he had already died from internal injuries and exposure. It was a courageous decision to send his companion out, for he must have realized his chances for survival were indeed grim. Although rare, such incidents underscore the seriousness of Rockies' caving. Rick was liked by all and he has left a huge gap in our small caving community.

Rather more accessible than our deepest and longest caves are the caves of the Crowsnest Pass, which can be reached in a day. Located in a remarkable alpine area under the looming bulk of Mount Ptolemy is a plateau riddled with holes resembling the craters of the moon. Almost 30 years of exploration have yielded several kilometres of passageways, mainly in two spectacular cave systems, Gargantua and Yorkshire Pot.

Gargantua, currently 6 km in length, contains some of the largest passages in the country. For example. while travelling through Boggle Alley your light beam becomes lost in the darkness against a vast roof span. The cave is ensconced behind a large broken cliff on the flank of Mount Ptolemy. Eyeholes of the upper entrance peer out of the cliff and often a steep traverse must be made across a snow slope to reach the entrance. I once lost it on this slope and careened down 250 m of snow desperately trying to steer through jutting cliff bands, and eventually came to a stop on an easier-angled snow slope.

Recently, a lower entrance to Gargantua has been discovered. We guide visitors through the cave from top to bottom now, rappelling five drops, pulling the rope down as we go to emerge from the snowbank close to where I finished falling—four hours underground. Actually, this is a very wet exit as the entrance is under a stream descending from the cliff, which runs beneath the snow. In years of high snowfall the exit may be blocked or be very tight, so we try to make sure it's open before we do our pull-down rope trips. Faced with trudging through heavy snow one October, I forestalled checking the bottom entrance and went for the pull-down trip. Three hours later, five of us arrived at the bottom only to find very heavy ice blocking the way out. Two hours with the ice axe and thoroughly wet, we had progressed some 3 m only to be faced with an impenetrable wall of ice. Daylight filtered in distantly. After free climbing some of the bottom pitches we finally were rescued the next day by a team that had camped at the entrance. A three hour trip had become a 22 hour trip!

Across the plateau beneath the cratered landscape lies Yorkshire Pot, a deep cave with many entrances now 14 km in length. In fact, each snow-filled crater (doline in karst terminology) feeds water to the cave during the summer melt. Most are blocked by frost-shattered rubble, but some are open and others have yielded to excavation. On occasional years, snow levels are so high that entrances never appear. On one winter expedition to Yorkshire Pot the party had to dig 10 m through snow to access the main entrance to the cave! Once inside any of Yorkshire's entrances, one is faced with a series of drops necessitating ropes, which take you down almost 400 m underground. The feeling of isolation is intense. It was on one exploration trip here that Bari Barabas, one of our part-time guides, dislocated her shoulder. Practically unaided, for her party could do little to help her, she was able to regain the surface after 12 gruelling hours. She had to operate the clamps for ascending the ropes (ascenders) and climb through strenuous squeezes. If you cannot self-rescue then the logistics multiply tenfold, as happened when someone fell 13 m close to the entrance of Yorkshire Pot. On that occasion the individual emerged from the cave on a stretcher 38 hours after entering it!

The top entrance to Gargantua Cave in the Crowsnest Pass caving area. Photo Dave Thomson.

Now Yorkshire Pot has a bottom entrance that goes by the name of Heave-Ho, suggestive of the extensive effort in excavating it. This entrance comes out in a picturesque alpine valley with a lake to the north of the plateau. Although many entrance-to-entrance trips are possible from any of the multiple entrances of Yorkshire Pot, the truly world-class, pull-down trip involving 13 rappels is from the main entrance to Heave-Ho.

Yorkshire Pot has well over 100 places where with careful looking new passages might be found. It may yet overtake Castleguard Cave in length. Naturally, the thrill of exploration takes cavers to the Crowsnest Pass every year.

These three examples of Rockies' caving paint a somewhat ideal picture of exploration and do not indicate the many trips made by cave enthusiasts where little is discovered. Sometimes morsels are hard-won, and we in the ASS have had our share. One winter we skied 50 km to a stream cave discovered by the inveterate Dave Thomson (Everyday Dave) one summer in Hamber Provincial Park, B.C. The idea was that unlike the summer, when Dave could not enter the cave owing to high water levels, the cave would be dry or the underground stream would be frozen. Our five day trip started in temperatures of -24°C and the temperature continuously dropped. I recount part of our third day from "Which Way to the North Pole?," an article I wrote for the *Canadian Caver*.

"When we reached the lake our worst fears were realized. The wind had not changed and was still blasting westwards down the ice creating snow

devils in its path. We put our heads down and headed up the mighty white strip of Fortress Lake, guarded by massive quartzite peaks such as the wedge-shaped Chizel Peak and Serenity Mountain. Himalayan-style snow plumes whirled from their summit ridges. We were frozen by the time the [ruined] cabin came up and rested briefly. The next section was endless and it was here that we became frostbitten: noses, faces and fingers. Never was there a more appropriate phrase than 'God, it's hell in the karst!'"

When we got back to the Icefields Parkway at 1:00 am after five days out in the elements, the temperature had dropped to -47°C. One of our cars had to be towed 5 km down the highway before it would start, and all of this for 100 m of passage! We returned to the cave one July for a week that was marked by seven

Looking into Close-to-the-Edge Cave, a shaft 254 m deep. Photo Ron Lacelle.

encounters with grizzly bears and the Icefields Parkway blocked by a freak snowstorm!

The history of modern exploration in the Canadian Rockies is a colourful one. I haven't mentioned Close-to-the-Edge with its 254 m-long entrance shaft that you could comfortably drop the Calgary Tower into. Recent exploration there has stopped at another huge shaft, giving hope that this cave will surpass Arctomys as the deepest cave in North America (north of the Mexican border, that is). Nor have we touched on the exquisite beauty of the ice caves—actually limestone caves whose walls and roof are adorned with an array of delicate ice crystals. And just a few caves are reasonably accessible like Rat's Nest Cave. There are none close to civilization that can match the richness of its resources.

CANADA'S TWELVE LONGEST AND DEEPEST CAVES (February, 1999)

Longest		
Cave	Location	Length (km)
1. Castleguard Cave	Columbia Icefield	20.1
2. Yorkshire Pot	Crowsnest Pass	13.8
3. Arch-Treasure Cave	Vancouver Island	8.1
4. Thanksgiving Cave	Vancouver Island	7.9
5. Ursa Major	Vancouver Island	6.2
6. Three Island Cave	Ottawa River	6.2
7. Gargantua	Crowsnest Pass	6.0
8. Weymer Cave System	Vancouver Island	5.4
9. Nakimu Caves	Glacier National Park	4.5
10. Windy Link Pot	Vancouver Island	4.4
11. Rat's Nest Cave	Bow Valley, Alberta	4.0
12. Sky Pot-Slot Canyon Cave	Vancouver Island	4.0

Deepest		
Cave	Location	Depth (m)
1. Arctomys	Mount Robson Prov. Park	536
2. Close-to-the-Edge	Dezaiko Ranges, B.C.	440
3. Thanksgiving Cave	Vancouver Island	394
4. Castleguard Cave	Columbia Icefield	390
5. Yorkshire Pot	Crowsnest Pass	389
6. Arch-Treasure Cave	Vancouver Island	352
7. Glory 'Ole	Vancouver Island	313
8. Q5	Vancouver Island	301
9. Gargantua	Crowsnest Pass	286
10. Weymer Cave System	Vancouver Island	273
11. Nakimu Caves	Glacier National Park	270
12. White Hole	Mount Bocock, B.C.	253
(Rat's Nest Cave is 245 m deep—ranking 14th)		

3 Geological Origin of the Cave Rock

It is 360 million years ago, at the end of the Devonian period. We are looking northwest across the ancient Panthalassan Ocean from the super-continent of Laurasia, formed by a collision of several continents with ancestral North America. Extensive reef building has taken place, and reef building will continue into the early Carboniferous period, ending about 320 million years ago. These reefs are tropical, for we are less than 200 km north of the equator, an equator being left behind as Laurasia shifts northward, predicating the onset of cooler climes.

Waves break over an offshore reef and the clear, warm water invites us to snorkle, especially as we are keen to see what's living there. However, snorkelling would likely be incredibly foolhardy, because there are large creatures in this sea. Some of them, such as ancestral sharks, are formidable indeed—perhaps numerous and aggressive in this pre-human world. Better we confine ourselves to the back-reef lagoons inaccessible to the really big marine predators.

Rat's Nest Cave will form some 300 million years later within these shallow marine deposits, although of course the sediments will be much changed by then. What we are seeing now is their deposition prior to being modified by titanic geological processes. The resulting rock layers formed will be known as the Livingstone and Mount Head formations, units sandwiched between other reef and shallow-marine deposits that will eventually make up the Rundle group of early Carboniferous age. (Impressive cliffs of these deposits tower over Canmore in the modern setting.)

As we float over the reefs, we observe numerous crinoids living there. We might call them "sea lilies," although they are not plants. They are animals: echinoderms, the same group as starfish and sea urchins. Feathery petals fan out from a cup-shaped calyx supported by a long stem. After death, only fragments of stems, which are made of stacked pill-like segments, will remain as fossils.

Bryozoans also make up a significant part of the reef. Coral-like but not truly corals, they grow in colonies that look like mosaics of a shattered window screen. True corals live here, too, and most of these are isolated horn (or rugose) corals seen dotting the reef.

Anchored to the reef are productid brachiopods filtering nutrients from the ocean as it heaves back and forth across the reef. These look like clams but are not related. Unlike a clamshell, the two parts of a brachiopod shell are of different sizes. The anchored, underlying shell is larger than the upper one, which opens during feeding. There are many fish in attendance and other creatures scuttling over the seabed among the anchored brachiopods, bryozoans and crinoids. However, only the animals such as the anchored species that secrete calcite as shells or body parts will be preserved as fossils in the cave walls.

The Livingstone and Mount Head formations also contain evidence of sponges and radiolaria, whose spicules and microscopic shells remain as flinty nodules of chert poking out from the cave walls. Three hundred million years of geological processes have placed these marine fossils in the cave walls at a great distance from the ocean and high above sea level.

An important event in those geological processes was the assembly of Pangea, a super-continent formed when Laurussia joined with Asia to become Laurasia, then joined with Gondwana (comprising Africa, South America, Antarctica and India) to form Pangea: all the world's continents in a single landmass. The region that would later become the Canadian Rockies lay on Pangea's western continental shelf, home to a rich assortment of marine plants and animals.

At the end of the Permian, around 245 million years ago, a massive extinction of life occurred—far greater than the famed dinosaur extinction—that resulted in the disappearance of 85 per cent of the world's species, compared to 65 per cent in the late Cretaceous dinosaur-extinction event. While an asteroid may have been responsible for the late Permian die-off as well as the late Cretaceous disaster, no evidence for a Permian impact has yet been found. An interesting alternative idea is the "suffocation hypothesis" that holds that as the oceans shrank at the expense of a growing landmass, oxygen liberated from the oceans was reduced. Carbon dioxide built up, owing in part to increased burning of vegetation on land, especially along drying shorelines. In this scenario there was less and less oxygen on the planet, causing loss of species.

Regardless of its cause, the Permian extinction marked the end of Paleozoic life, which had started in the Cambrian period 543 million years before. Mesozoic life began with the Triassic period 245 million years ago. Four unrelated groups of reptiles colonized the single ocean of Panthalassan at this time.

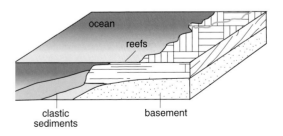

Figure 3.1. Geological situation during the Carboniferous period prior to mountain building.

The late Permian and early Triassic also saw a phase of gentle uplift pushing the shoreline eastward. This briefly exposed the marine sediments, including the upper layers of the Rundle group and the overlying Permian rock, some of which were lost to erosion. Subsidence followed, allowing the sea to once again cover the region. Triassic shallow-water sediments of the Spray River group accumulated.

The Jurassic and Cretaceous periods were next, starting some 208 million years ago. At this time the super-continent of Pangea was breaking apart. Beginning in the mid-Jurassic, around 180 million years ago, the Atlantic Ocean began to open, splitting Pangea and pushing North America westward. Through the rest of the Jurassic, the Cretaceous and into the Tertiary periods, North America moved farther and farther west over the floor of the Pacific Ocean. Large volcanic islands had formed as magma punched through the oceanic crust. As the continent bulldozed into these islands, both the islands and the edge of the continent crumpled adding the island landmasses onto western North America and producing the Columbia, Omineca and Cassiar mountains to the west.

By 140 million years ago the western part of the Rockies was standing tall, but the Canmore area was under water. Down warping east of the new mountain ranges had created an inland sea that received extensive sediments from the rising mountains of British Columbia. At Canmore and Banff, late Jurassic and early Cretaceous sandstone and shale deposits contain coal from long-dead forests that thrived on the shoreline deltas of that time. This shallow sea, fringed with huge marshes and tidal flats along with the warm climatic conditions at the time, were the scene for a profusion of life, which included the largest land animals ever to roam the earth: the dinosaurs.

About 85 million years ago in the late Cretaceous, the Front Ranges of the Rockies began to rise. This last phase of mountain building saw massive compression and faulting of the reef limestone and the inland-sea sediments to form the mountains of the Front Ranges, including the Canmore area, and later the foothills to the east. This process was more of an "up piling" or stacking, rather than uplift, giving the Rockies the appearance of books fallen sideways in a partly filled bookcase.

The inland-sea was drained during the resultant uplift, and the thick slab of Carboniferous limestone (later to host Rat's Nest Cave) was pushed northeastward over Mesozoic sandstone and shale. The faulting that

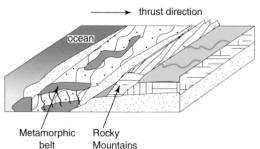

thrust direction

Figure 3.2. Mountain building phase during the early Cretaceous to the early Tertiary (85-45 million years ago).

Metamorphic belt

Rocky Mountains

occurred during the compression of the limestone yielded lines of weakness, along one of which Rat's Nest Cave eventually formed. This takes us to the next installment of the geological story, the geological history of the cave itself.

GEOLOGICAL EVENTS UP TO THE BUILDING OF THE CANADIAN ROCKY MOUNTAINS

Eon/Era	Million of Years Ago	Event
Hadean eon		
	[a] 4600	Earth forms by accretion.
	4000-3500	First stirring of life (single cell).
Archean	3200	Cyanobacteria appear (stromatolites).
	2900-1800	Canadian Rockies basement rocks form.
Proterozoic	1900-900	Supercontinent of Rodinia forms.
	800-544	Rodinia splits up.
		Massive extinction occurs.
Paleozoic era		
Cambrian	544-510	Rapid diversification of life. Burgess Shales form.
Ordovician	510-441	Margin of ocean has moved inland.
Silurian	441-410	Mild uplift, ocean recedes.
Devonian	410-353	Return of the ocean and extensive reef building. Extinction at the end of this period.
Carboniferous	353-300	Ocean advances. **Cave-hosting limestone forms.**
Permian	300-250	Uplift of the Appalachians. Most massive extinction to date. Eighty-eight per cent of species disappear.
Mesozoic era		
	250-65	Supercontinent of Pangea breaks up. Atlantic Ocean opens. North America moves northwest. Formation of coal in the Banff-Canmore area.
Jurassic	175	Mountain building in Canada west of Rockies.
Cretaceous	166	Fifty per cent extinction (including dinosaurs) by large impact.
	140-45	Canadian Rockies form. **Cave-forming faults active.**

4 Geological History of Rat's Nest Cave

The extensive faulting referred to in the previous chapter provided the subterranean paths for groundwater to travel. For example, the hot water feeding the nearby Cave and Basin Hot Springs at Banff comes up from deep underground along such faults and associated fractures.

When we talk of groundwater flow in the Rocky Mountains, we must also take into account the rivers and multiple glaciations that have carved the mountains into their present-day shapes. The caves have resulted from this combination of faulting, river erosion and glaciation.

In middle Eocene time, around 45 million years ago, the Canadian Rocky Mountains were more rounded, with winding, V-shaped valleys. It wasn't until the Pliocene starting around 4.9 million years ago that glaciations started to significantly change the landscape, albeit at higher elevations. During the great Pleistocene glaciations, over the last 1.65 million years, the valleys as well as the mountains were greatly modified by moving ice. Major glacial advances eroded the sides of the mountains, straightened the valleys and widened them, producing Matterhorn-like peaks, sawtooth ridges, huge cliffs and deep U-shaped valleys. With the extensive topographic relief and the huge volumes of water associated with the glaciers, a complex subterranean plumbing system developed.

The drainage story starts with rivers flowing eastward from rising mountain ranges west of the Canmore area, before Grotto Mountain and the rest of the Front Ranges existed. The major river systems of the Rockies—for example, the Athabasca, North Saskatchewan and Bow—were powerful enough eroders to hold their courses as the Front Ranges began to rise across their paths about 85 million years ago (known as antecedent drainage). Perhaps caves started to form in the Front Ranges at this time, but they would not have survived the tortured folding and fracturing of the rock caused by mountain building. It wasn't until Miocene time, 24 million years ago and well after mountain building tapered off, that Rat's Nest could develop.

There has been a great deal of erosion since the beginning of the Miocene, leaving cave segments at the top of mountain ridges. I have seen this extensively in the Crowsnest Pass area, and recently have had occasion to see it above Johnston Canyon in the Sawback Range, where there is a new cave discovery. The cave is at an elevation of about 2500 m, and passes right through a high, rocky spur. It must have formed below the water

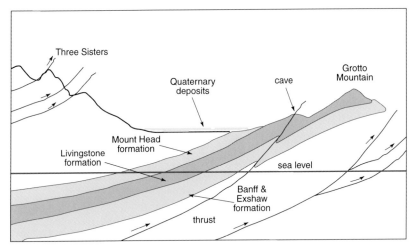

Figure 4.1. Geological cross-section of the Bow Valley in the vicinity of Rat's Nest Cave.

table, which is today below the level of the valley floor. The valleys have since been eroded downward to elevations of 1000-1500 m. I've also found isolated cave remnants high in ridges on Mount Isabelle in Kootenay National Park, and near the town of Cadomin, just east of Jasper National Park. Other remnants have been reported near the summit of Leyland Mountain at over 2400 m. Interestingly, some of these caves contain sediments that appear to originate from areas far to the west suggestive of extensive ancestral drainage developed during the Miocene.

Another feature that suggests the co-genesis of some caves with rivers in the Rocky Mountains is the tendency to find fossil cave systems high above large river gaps, places where rivers have cut through mountain ranges. The caves are "fossil" because they no longer serve as major subterranean drains. We can find fossil caves along many of the main river valleys, and Rat's Nest Cave is one such, found at the east end of Grotto Mountain just before the Bow cuts eastward through the Fairholme Range.

A very brief history of Rat's Nest Cave would go something like this:

In Miocene time the early Bow River flowed between the Rundle and Fairholme ranges. Groundwater circulated in adjacent faults, along one of which Rat's Nest Cave began to be dissolved out. The passages were water-filled and probably not large enough for humans—if they had been around at that time and equipped with scuba gear—to explore.

The cave-forming process continued slowly for millions of years, until the Pleistocene ice ages, when it sped up considerably. During each ice advance a mountain glacier flowed down the Bow Valley, widening it, straightening it and cutting new gaps through the ridges. This changed the course of the river that followed the valley between glaciations; at one stage the Bow River flowed out of the mountains along Lake Minnewanka and into the Ghost River. At another time it followed its present course, but instead of going through the gap at Exshaw it appears to have flowed directly over Skogan Pass south of Pigeon Mountain and into the drainage of today's Kananaskis River.

During the greatest of the Pleistocene glaciations, the Bow Glacier was at least a kilometre thick. Rat's Nest Cave was likely most active at this time, carrying copious quantities of glacial water through Grotto Mountain. (The cave would be referred to as an ice-contact cave at this point in its development.) The Bow Glacier advanced and retreated at least four times, and during the melting phases would have delivered vast amounts of water to the cave. We see sediments and mud-lined walls inside the cave as evidence of this.

The final phase of cave development occurred as the Bow Glacier was in its last retreat about 12,000-13,000 years ago. The cave passages drained, and Rat's Nest was left high and dry, 180 m above the valley floor.

Actually, it is not strictly correct to say that the cave is "fossil," as today we find springs down at the level of the Bow River that seem to carry water from the cave. However, the few streams encountered in the cave are underfit: trickles compared to the massive flows the cave once took.

The next chapter looks at the research I have undertaken at the cave and we shall see how this model for cave formation or speleogenesis is supported.

GEOLOGICAL EVENTS SINCE THE BUILDING OF THE CANADIAN ROCKY MOUNTAINS

Era/Period	Thousands of Years Ago	Event
Mesozoic era		
	250,000-65,000	Supercontinent of Pangea breaks up. Atlantic Ocean opens. North America moves northwest. Formation of coal in the Banff-Canmore area.
Jurassic	175,000	Mountain building west of Rockies.
Cretaceous	66,000	Fifty per cent extinction (including dinosaurs) by large impact.
	140,000-45,000	Canadian Rockies form. **Cave-forming faults created.**
Cenozoic era		
Tertiary	66,000-1600	Mountain building tapers off.
	24,000-1650	**Groundwater starts to enlarge faults and form cave.**
Quaternary	1650-present	Earth climate cools, ice ages begin.
Pleistocene	1650-1.1	Glaciers in the Rockies. **Cave greatly enlarged by glacial meltwater.** Mineral deposits accumulate.
Holocene	1.1-present	Human habitation in the Bow corridor. Cave finally drained of glacial water. Deposits (minerals, bones and artifacts) accumulate.

5 Ancient Environments: What the Cave Can Tell Us

The cave walls tell their own story...

It seems that the initial skeleton of Rat's Nest Cave formed as water began to move slowly through a substantial fault system in the limestone, gradually widening some of its fractures over long periods of time. Study of the geological history tells us that the rock was broken to form the fault during the most recent phase of mountain building in the Rockies. This episode began about 85 million years ago during the late Cretaceous, and ended during the mid-Eocene, about 45 million years ago. The main fracture appears to be a thrust fault, which is very low-angled and hard to distinguish from the major bedding planes in the limestone, most of which will also have suffered lateral movement. During the orogeny (mountain building), part of the earth's crust known as an oceanic plate moved from the west, colliding with the North American continental plate, and causing the limestone and other sedimentary rocks to be pushed eastward. Squeezed against the relatively immovable continent, horizontal beds of sedimentary rock along the coastal area had nowhere to go but upward. The malleable rock beds first buckled until they could buckle no further. They were then fractured and faulted to form stacks—looking perhaps as books do when they lean against one another in an unfilled bookshelf. Millions of years of erosion reduced this buckled and broken mass of rock beds into the west-east sawtooth profile we see today.

However, water probably did not begin to exploit the thrust fault until much later, perhaps sometime during the Miocene epoch, which began some 24 million years ago. Such exploitation began at about the same time that the course of the Bow River was being imprinted upon a former landscape high above the level of the modern valley floor. Assuming that the valley has been down cut by 0.15 to 0.50 m every thousand years (figures commonly quoted for the Canadian Rocky Mountains), this imprinting must have started at least 12 million years ago.

Knowing that rivers flow happily on the rock surface for millions of years, an obvious question is, "Why did water flow along the thrust fault in the first place?" The real answer is very complex, and hinges upon processes that affected the rocks in the distant past. In simple terms though, the water was able to penetrate and enlarge the fracture because it provided a plane of weakness in the otherwise solid mass of limestone bedrock. Most rainfall and snow—together known as precipitation—and the groundwater from which it forms, are slightly acidic. The acid groundwater comes about when carbon dioxide gas from the atmosphere or from pores in the soil

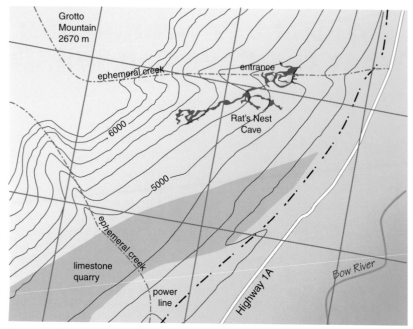

Figure 5.1. Map of cave area with cave shown in silhouette.

dissolves in the originally neutral water to form carbonic acid. Though very "weak" compared to many other acids, the carbonic acid is able to attack and dissolve limestone, and it slowly enlarges any cavities it passes through.

To the modern speleologist, the earliest underground course followed by the water would be known as an inception route, in line with a concept advanced by Dr. Dave Lowe of the British Geological Survey, who is also the editor of a journal called *Cave and Karst Science*. Now inception horizons are features within the rock succession, usually related to the beds themselves, where cave formation is originated. Such horizons are connected by steep fracture planes or, more rarely, by low-angle fractures such as the thrust fault in Rat's Nest Cave. In some cases it is difficult to tell the difference between a true low-angle fracture and an inception horizon bedding-plane across which relative slippage has occurred as the rock was folded.

The reasons why cave development starts along a particular feature, or set of features, are very complicated. In 1991, Art Palmer, a well-known cave scientist from the USA, wrote, "The origin of a limestone cave hangs by a delicate thread." He was referring to the lottery-like odds against all the potential contributory factors being favourable at the same time! It all depends upon just the right combination of rock structures (beds, joints, fractures and faults), rock type (not only limestone, but also its relationship to adjacent rocks such as shale or sandstone) and the complex chemical reactions that are localized along most inception horizons. In the earliest stages not only carbonic acid is involved—it may well be that other acids played a very significant part at this time. For example, sulphide minerals can be oxidized to produce sulphuric acid as water passes through rock horizons that contain them. Rat's Nest Cave shows good evidence for the active involvement of all of these features.

Use of the ideas developed within the inception horizon hypothesis helps us to view caves in their natural perspective. In the past we have tended to approach cave science in a very anthropocentric way, formulating our ideas on the basis of caves that we can enter. In fact, when we enter a cave, we see it only in its extreme maturity or old age. Most of the cave's history has taken place when openings were only a few millimetres wide, or initially much less. Time scales of cave development are now conceived to be in the order of tens, hundreds or even thousands of times greater than was thought in the early days of speleology. In some cases it can be shown that inception occurred at the same time as the parent rock was forming (syngluesis).

Today Rat's Nest Cave is slowly but surely passing through its old age phase. Not only are its passages big enough to be entered, but the eroding water that once flowed through them, and sometimes entirely filled the cave, is now absent. In most parts of the cave we can plainly see the major weakness along which the water first passed. Erosion of the thrust fault has produced passages with an overall lenticular cross-section, though in detail the walls are sculpted into intricate patterns of depressions, pockets, flutes and tubes, called speleogens. Superficially similar features seen in fast-flowing surface rivers and creeks are generally formed by mechanical erosion (corrasion). Rock is actually worn away by water-transported abrasive sediment, especially by the trundling of cobbles along the riverbeds. Common features such as mill-holes are formed in this way. Comparable features can be seen in caves, especially where there are fast flowing underground streams. However, most of these are formed largely by the attack of acidic groundwater upon the bedrock. As mentioned, limestone is especially susceptible, as it is quite soluble, even in weak acids.

Where water originally entered the Rat's Nest Cave thrust fault is unknown, and the earliest drainage could have originated on land surfaces long since removed by erosion. Nonetheless, the cave sections now visible at lower levels were dissolved out from the tiny fault fractures to form passages of human proportions. What can we say about the past water flows or, as it is referred to, the paleohydrology? Some wall depressions, each shaped like the bowl of a spoon, are known as solution scallops, or simply scallops. These can tell us not only how fast the water flowed through the cave passages, but also, because scallops are not symmetrical, in which direction the water moved. Details of past flow directions are commonly not obvious in a cave. Especially during the early stages of development most of the activity takes place beneath the water table, where flow can actually be "uphill," depending upon the pressure head and confinement of the water within favourable parts of the rock sequence. Examples of flow scallops can be seen

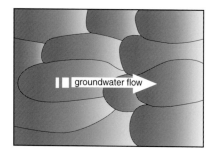

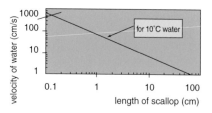

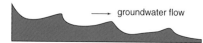

Figure 5.2. Solution scallops indicate original direction of water flow.

right at the Rat's Nest Cave entrance, where water once cascaded down a slab and out into the canyon. Of course, the direction here is obvious, but the scallops provide a satisfying confirmation of the relationship between limestone dissolution and turbulent water flow. These scallops are about 5 cm across and the steepest faces of the scallop depressions are on the upstream side. The small diameter is indicative of fast flow, as the larger the scallop diameter, the slower was the water flow that formed them. The mathematical relationship (which is termed "inverse logarithmic") is known from observation, but is not well understood theoretically. In this case the speed of flow would have been around 40 cm/second, which is what might be expected for water tumbling down a 30° slab.

Caver Tom Miller in Yorkshire Pot. The flow was around 10-20 cm/second in the picture.

Deeper inside the cave, in large passages (for example, those beyond the Slimy Climb), there are wall depressions measuring almost a metre across. Whereas evidence of the former flow direction is ambiguous in this instance, the speed of flow can be estimated at about 1 cm/second, which is very slow. Because the ceilings as well as the walls are scalloped, we know that water must have completely filled the passageways, which have diameters of 3 m or more. A rough calculation shows water could have moved through these passageways at a rate of 100 litres/second. The cave has several parallel passages, possibly including some as yet undiscovered, so the cave probably transmitted a great deal more, perhaps as much as 1000 litres or one tonne of water every second. These caves are large natural pipes! One of the largest springs in the Rockies, at Maligne Canyon in Jasper National Park, has been recorded to discharge a mind-boggling 40 tonnes of water per second, most of it coming underground from Medicine Lake, which has no overland outflow.

Where scallops showing an obvious flow direction are exposed in Rat's Nest Cave, it is clear the ancient groundwater came from the northwest, travelling more or less in the same direction as the Bow River. What is most impressive is that at the northern end of the cave the water rose under pressure from a depth of 150 m before flowing down through the cave. It moved upward again through the pit by the present entrance, and on downward through the Grottos, to a final siphon that lies 245 m below the highest point in the cave. The modern entrance represents a later breach that was cut into the buried "pipe" sometime during the last glacial retreat, when huge torrents of sediment-laden water from decaying ice-sheets cut side canyons all along the Bow Valley. "Upstream" exploration of the cave has presently ended at the bottom of the original 150 m "lift," known as the Ignominious End, where the passage is blocked by sediments. This point is deep inside Grotto Mountain, so where on earth (literally!) did the cave-forming water originate?

Steve Worthington, a fellow PhD graduate of McMaster University in Ontario, studied the hydrology of various Rocky Mountain springs in the Crowsnest Pass area. Worth visiting is the Crowsnest Spring itself, which can be seen from the highway to be spewing out huge volumes of water into Crowsnest Lake. The water here rises from an unknown depth. Tom Barton, one of the explorers of the underwater passages in Rat's Nest Cave, scuba dived the spring to a depth of 40 m, the safe recreational diving limit. He stopped his descent, hovering over an ominously descending blackness. Steve studied this spring as well as others in the area. He measured chemistry, temperature and flow, and found that water could have entered the spring network from more than 100 km away. By measuring the amount of sulphate dissolved in the water, Steve was able to show the water flow was deep enough to allow calcium sulphate (mineral anhydrite) to be dissolved from underlying evaporitic beds. Nearby, at the Banff Hot Springs, we see water emerging from an estimated depth of 2 to 3 km, with an ultimate source that is very distant. This water also dissolves calcium sulphate from deeply buried evaporitic beds. As the mineral-laden water rises

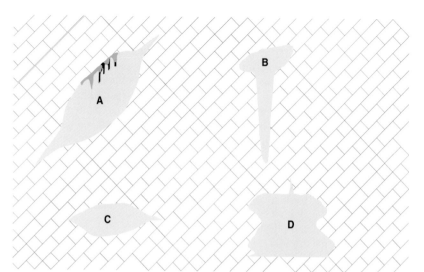

Figure 5.3. *Typical passage cross sections:* **A**. *Phreatic tube developed on a dipping bedding plane or fault;* **B**. *Keyhole;* **C**. *As in A, but horizontal;* **D**. *Tube formed on a horizontal bedding or fault with a vertical joint in the ceiling.*

toward the surface, sulphur-reducing bacteria feed on the dissolved sulphate, producing hydrogen sulphide that is subsequently oxidized to form sulphuric acid.

So, it may be that Rat's Nest Cave is part of a very much longer cave system and to date only the tip of the proverbial iceberg has been located and explored. Steve Worthington's theories regarding underground flow regimes in the limestone and dolomite of the Canadian Rocky Mountains suggest that more than 50 km of passageways could exist beyond the currently known 4 km of Rat's Nest Cave. Accepting this possibility, and considering the known lateral extent of the thrust fault system, the water could have entered the cave from as far away as Lake Minnewanka, a straight-line distance of 25 km. As things stand it seems that water must at least have passed right through Grotto Mountain, with the nearest known sink point in Cougar Canyon, 5 km away at Canmore. What a phenomenal journey through the mountain that would be if we could only follow the ancient watercourse!

We know that Rat's Nest Cave formed entirely below the water table, in what is known as the phreatic zone. Cave development generally begins here, but most caves are modified later, when water tables fall owing to external factors such as valley incision, uplift or glacial retreat. Cascading streams above the falling water table, in the so-called vadose zone, modify the earlier passageways by entrenching their floors. Deep, steep-sided canyons are cut beneath the original tube-like phreatic passages, and keyhole-shaped profiles result. Several kilometres of such canyon passages, some entrenched more than 25 m beneath the floors of the original phreatic tubes, are found in Castleguard, Canada's longest cave, which starts beneath the Columbia Icefield.

Only minor sections of floor entrenchment are found in Rat's Nest Cave, where most passages are free of any sign of vadose incision. Somehow the water-filled cave was able to drain so rapidly that there was little time for entrenchment by vadose streams. Drainage of the cave probably occurred in response to the rapid retreat of the Bow Glacier. Geologically speaking, this event was almost instantaneous, and it dropped the water table some 180 m to the valley bottom, while also removing the water source that fed the cave. Though powerful streams from ice sheets decaying on the mountain flanks cut steep canyons, one of which breached a buried cave passage to form the present entrance, this water never penetrated significantly into the cave. Rat's Nest and similar caves are termed ice contact caves, formed as water from the base of a glacier—in this case the Bow Glacier—was injected into the bedrock. In this situation, with ice thickness a kilometre or more overlying the cave, water tables rise to very high levels, supporting cave development in the phreatic zone. Of course, such an enormous thickness of ice produces intense pressure heads, capable of driving water hundreds of metres both upward and downward through the rock.

What about some of the other features displayed in the walls of Rat's Nest Cave? Many passage walls and especially passage ceilings contain deep cavities or pockets. Almost invariably these pockets end at narrow cracks, or are developed along tiny crack lines. The phenomenon is not rare, as it can be found in caves throughout the world, but their occurrence remained a puzzle for many years. Then, in 1964 an eminent Swiss speleologist, the late Alfred Bögli, came up with an explanation, which he described as mischungskorrosion or mixing corrosion.

According to Bögli's theory, the chemistry of water seeping downward through cracks in the bedrock is unlike that of the water flowing through the main cave conduits. Seepage water originates from the biologically active soil zone and is initially highly charged with carbon dioxide, making it capable of dissolving limestone, or aggressive. However, this carbonic acid soon becomes neutralized as it passes through, and dissolves, the limestone. When it reaches an underlying cave passage the seepage water is already saturated with calcium carbonate and incapable of further dissolution. Water flowing along the passageways was in any case initially less aggressive than the seepage water, as it did not have the benefit of contact with soil carbon dioxide. But, just like the seepage waters from above, such flowing waters are also saturated with calcium carbonate at the point where they meet. Amazingly, however, as these two saturated waters mix, the mixture becomes aggressive and pocket formation takes place. Why should this be?

In simple terms, the answer is that as more and more carbon dioxide is added to water, the amount of acidity increase reduces. The relationship between the amount of dissolved carbon dioxide and acidity of the solution is not in direct proportion, and does not plot out graphically as a straight line. Because of this non-linear relationship, the acidity of the resultant mixture can be enhanced when two waters carrying initially different concentrations of carbon dioxide mix together.

The mixing corrosion process can usefully be invoked to explain caves that formed without obvious links to the surface, where entrances are only exposed by later erosion. In fact, the concept has proved invaluable in supporting advances right across the branch of cave science that deals with cave development, commonly known as speleogenesis. Mixing corrosion effects are also produced in other situations, involving variations in water chemistry either unrelated or only partly related to carbon dioxide. For example, in some coastal areas enhanced limestone dissolution is achieved by the mixing of fresh and saline water; elsewhere the combined effects of sulphuric and carbonic acids in cave waters have been recognized.

Back in Rat's Nest Cave, just before the descending passage called the Laundry Chute, a complex of tubes leads off in all directions, and one of these has curious bedrock projections hanging from its ceiling. Referred to as pendants, such projections commonly develop after a passage has been infilled by sediment deposits. In Rat's Nest Cave the sediments were glacial in nature, and were injected into the cave by streams running under the ice sheets. As the sediments are deposited they protect (or armour) passage floors and walls, preventing them from being dissolved away. Flow can continue at the ceiling level for some time, until eventually the passage locally becomes completely blocked. As the passage cross-section becomes more restricted, both the pressure head and the speed of flow increase. In fingering its way between the sediments and the ceiling the water dissolves out a series of braided (anastomosing) channels, looking something like the distributaries in a surface stream. The braids become deeper and change position with time, so that eventually a series of rocky pendants (like pointed moguls) is left projecting from the ceiling, where they can be exposed by subsequent removal of the sediment under changed drainage conditions.

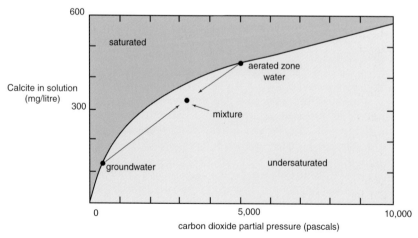

Figure 5.4. Mixing curve for saturated and unsaturated groundwater. The figure shows that when two saturated waters of differing composition mix, the mixture can become unsaturated (acidic) and can once again dissolve the limestone bedrock.

Cave pendants on the ceiling of a cave passage indicating it was once filled with sediments. Photo Tony White.

Interesting caves are found near the Svartisen Glacier close to the Arctic Circle in Norway. Stein-Erik Lauritzen, an eminent speleologist from the University of Bergen, has extensively studied the paleohydrology of these caves because of their link to the large glacier system. One such cave is no longer connected to the glacier streams, but at one stage powerful flows of water must have passed around a mound of sediment in the centre of a passage. An astonishing array of pendants has been formed, covering all of the walls and the ceiling. These pendants are fingerlike, more than 30 cm long, and cut from brilliant white marble—a truly outstanding example. The armouring effect of inwashed sediment and the subsequent generally upward dissolutional effects on exposed bedrock surfaces are referred to as paragenesis. Surface-derived sediments that have entered Rat's Nest Cave during several distinct episodes have later been flushed out again, and this leads us to the next part of the story.

The cave mineral story...

We have talked about rock sediments that were flushed into the cave by glacial meltwaters, but what of the mineral sediments (speleothems) that are formed by drip water after the main flow has gone? Speleothems are essentially the limestone bedrock dissolved by seeping groundwater, brought into the open cave and re-precipitated as calcite, a pure form of calcium carbonate ($CaCO_3$). Fortunately, the age of many of these minerals can be measured, at least as far back as 400,000 years old, and greater ages can be estimated, to perhaps 750,000 years ago. This covers just under half of the time that has passed since the first great glaciers came and went during the Pleistocene epoch.

Column formation showing tens of thousands of years of growth. Photo John Gunn.

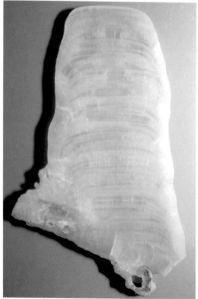

Sectioned stalagmite showing growth layers. Photo Yavor Shopov.

The dating method takes advantage of the presence of trace amounts of radioactive uranium trapped within the crystalline speleothems. Being soluble, small quantities of uranium-rich minerals in the bedrock dissolve and travel in the groundwater, along with the calcium carbonate. Eventually the mineral-laden groundwater enters an air-filled passage, and the calcite is precipitated, along with the radioactive impurities, to produce the well-known mineral formations such as stalagmites and stalactites.

Concentrations of two uranium isotopes (^{234}U and ^{235}U) are measured. Each of these isotopes decays to form a distinct "daughter" product, and the concentrations of these, which are actually isotopes of thorium and protactinium (^{230}Th and ^{231}Pa), are also measured. The beauty of the method is that thorium and protactinium are both effectively insoluble, so that the uranium travels from its point of dissolution to its site of deposition uncontaminated by any pre-existing daughter products. Once the uranium has been locked into the speleothem mineral, new levels of thorium and protactinium daughters begin to build up. All of the isotopes are radioactive, so their concentrations can be measured by counting the alpha particles that they emit. Alternatively, their levels can be measured more accurately using a mass spectrometer. Knowing the half-life of their decays and the measured concentrations of the isotopes, we can calculate the age of the deposit. Of these two dating methods, the ^{234}U to ^{230}Th decay gives the most reliable results.

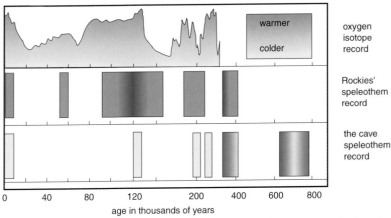

Figure 5.5. Speleothem dates from Rat's Nest Cave compared to other cave sites in the Canadian Rockies and the oxygen isotope record derived from deep sea and ice cores.

Cave scientists usually select a stalagmite or flowstone for dating. This is done with a strong environmental ethic in mind, attempting to make as little visible impact as possible on the cave. These types of deposits display broad, well-defined layering, from which it is straightforward to select a group of layers for dating after the speleothem has been cut in half along its axis of growth. Not only does bisecting the deposit show the banding well, but it also allows different tests to be made on each half: dating on one and climate studies on the other, but more on climate later.

Dates from Rat's Nest Cave have proved to be very important, because of the general scarcity of reliable dates relating to the regional glaciations. Each successive glacial advance down the Bow Valley partially or completely obliterated the deposits left by earlier advances. Surviving fragments of evidence are hard to piece together and are commonly ambiguous. In contrast, the cave has preserved information about past climatic events, in the form of sediment sequences, whether of mineral or glacial origin. Dated events recorded in the cave appear to relate to the four major glacial advance episodes that have been recognized in the Bow Valley corridor. Only a few dates are so far available, but their range (from 3800 years back to 766,000 years) bodes well for further useful results being obtained from the material still awaiting analysis. Even at this early stage the suite of ages recorded is equal to any yet found in other Canadian caves. Rat's Nest Cave may yet yield the most complete Quaternary record of any site in the region, cave or otherwise.

Significant gaps in the dating record indicate that speleothems did not grow during the glacial advances when the ground was frozen under permafrost, which shut down the source of mineral-laden seepage water. Alternatively, the cave may have been completely flooded by glacial water. In agreement with other Pleistocene glacial records, results confirm that the Rat's Nest Cave deposits formed only during interglacial periods, when the ground was not completely frozen or the cave flooded.

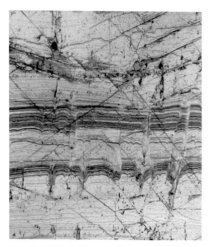

Detail of growth layers in flowstone. Layers represent hundreds or thousands of years.

Stalactite 881010 is especially interesting, because its minerals encapsulate details of so much recent geological history. It started life about 600,000 years ago as a tiny stalactite hanging naturally from the ceiling. During an undetermined period it thickened and grew to be about 0.5 m long, or perhaps even longer. We don't know for sure how long it became, because about 210,000 years ago the cave passage became flooded. Under the water, 881010 began to dissolve away, until the floodwaters finally receded leaving what was left of the stalactite with a thin coating of mud. Similar flood events happened at least four times during a 30,000-year period, until the stalactite's attachment eventually dissolved away and 881010 fell to the floor. At least one more flood occurred, adding another mud coating to the stalactite, and there it lay for another 180,000 years. About 4000 years ago, in the mid Holocene, long after the retreat of the last great ice sheet, things became exciting again for 881010 when a small stalagmite that looked like a fried egg grew on its top side. Then, even more recently, Homo sapiens did all sorts of unmentionable things to the stalactite to find out the details of its life story. Apart from anything else, in geological terms it suffered unimaginably rapid transport 3000 km eastward to McMaster University in Ontario, where it was dissected and dated.

Ocean sediments record evidence of a warm period that began around 245,000 years ago and lasted for about 60,000 years. The warmest conditions were during the 25,000 years from 210,000 to 185,000 years ago—the time during which the cyclical flood events at Rat's Nest Cave occurred. There is an intriguing possibility that these periodic inundations occurred when the Bow River was dammed by glacial outwash material and its flow was diverted northward, through Lake Minnewanka and into the prairies via the Ghost River valley. Evidence of this event is recognized in the local glacial record, but details of when it occurred are unknown. The information, provided by the Rat's Nest Cave stalactite, therefore offers a possible answer.

Another important speleothem is 881020, a 1 cm-thick piece of calcite flooring that overlies thinly banded mud. Mineral-laden water oozed over this mud bank 123,000 years ago, leaving the calcite crust. This date happens to correspond precisely with the end of the so-called Illinoian Glacial (named from the Great Lakes region), an age that is supported by dating evidence from ocean sediments and coral reef terraces. Such coral reef terraces are now found 5-10 m above modern sea level, implying that extensive melting of the ice caps at that time caused a significant sea level rise. Although our present interglacial is unusually warm (human factors excepted!), 123,000 years ago the climate was even warmer—actually being the warmest time during the Pleistocene glaciations. The delicate mud layers overlain by 881020 may well yield crucial regional information about events leading up to this warming maximum. Study has not yet started, but it will be interesting, for example, to look for pollen grains (palynology) and deduce what kind of vegetation grew in the Rocky Mountains 123,000 years ago.

Varieties of stalactites. Photo Dave Thomson.

No speleothems that grew during the last three glacial advances, spanning 75,000 to less than 18,000 years ago, have been found in the Rocky Mountains. This regional lack of speleothem growth testifies to the intensity of this last glaciation, with ice more than a kilometre thick over the site of modern Canmore. Let's hope it doesn't happen again soon!

The age dating research continues at the cave, which gives vitality to our interpretation. Currently, Feride Serefidin, a PhD student from McMaster University under Professor Derek Ford, is developing a dating program for a number of North American caves, in which Rat's Nest Cave features prominently.

Modern Minerals and Climatic Change...

The final part of the dating story lies in the Holocene, the modern epoch that began after the last glacial retreat (the end of the late Wisconsin glaciation). Speleothems have provided Holocene dates starting at around 10,000 years ago going right up to the present day, when the speleothems are still actually forming. Climate forecasters are very interested in climatic changes in the recent past. By using such information from around the world, and developing global computer models for past patterns of climatic change, they try to predict future change and attempt to measure human impacts upon it. The information they use comes from various geological sources, which are referred to collectively as proxy climate records. Until recently the most important ones have been from deep-sea foraminifera and polar ice cores. But these records relate to marine and polar situations. Increasingly, continental records are sought, and these include peat or lake-sediment cores and, yes, cave deposits.

In an attempt to contribute to this worldwide forum on climate reconstruction, Holocene speleothems from Rat's Nest Cave have been analyzed. Firstly, we have tried to improve the precision of the results by using carbon-14 dating. (The province of Alberta has an appropriate dating laboratory in Vegreville.) Secondly, we have made an isotopic analysis of the speleothem calcite, which tells us something about the paleoenvironment (past conditions of precipitation, vegetation cover and temperature). Thirdly, we have looked at a phenomenon known as luminescence, which can be observed in the calcite when it is subjected to bright light in the visible spectrum. Believe it or not, such luminescence appears to relate to past solar activity (sunspot cycles, intensity and so on). The sun's intensity affects the production of organic acids, which subsequently pass into the groundwater and are trapped in the cave minerals. It is this trapped organic material that gives rise to luminescence. So finely can the instruments be tuned that it is now possible to observe the effects of changes in the sun's strength from summer to winter over single-year periods.

Carbon-14 dating of speleothems is problematical, because they contain carbon from two sources: one, from dissolved calcium carbonate (limestone) and two, from soil and/or atmospheric carbon dioxide. The limestone contains no carbon-14, because it is so old that any original radiocarbon has been transformed to other isotopes by radioactive decay. The carbon from soil or atmospheric carbon dioxide does contain carbon-14, which is produced continuously in the upper atmosphere. Therefore, providing that the age of the speleothem does not exceed the limits of the dating method (about 50,000 years), its carbon-14 content can be measured and a date of deposition calculated. The problem is that so-called "dead" carbon derived

Ancient redissolved stalagmites. Melted shapes indicate these formations have spent time underwater during glacial cave flooding. Photo Dave Thomson.

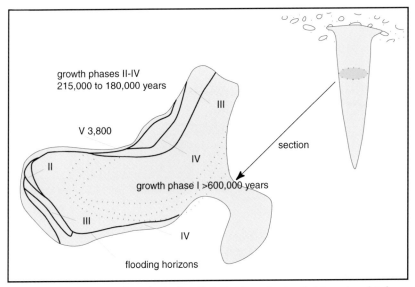

growth phases II-IV
215,000 to 180,000 years

III

V 3,800

section

IV

II

growth phase I >600,000 years

III

IV

flooding horizons

Figure 5.6. A cross-section of a stalactite from Rat's Nest Cave showing that it was inundated when the cave flooded several times during past glaciations.

from the limestone adds to the ratio of dead/live carbon, yielding ages that are too great. Two techniques have been used to recover the correct dates. Measurement of modern, actively forming speleothems, which should have zero-age, generally gives age values of around 4000 years. Some young speleothems have also been dated by the uranium-thorium methods described above. Similar discrepancies were found by both methods, suggesting that 4000 years is the right amount to subtract from the "false" dates.

Calcite ($CaCO_3$) also contains other isotopes of carbon and isotopes of oxygen that are not radioactive. Geological processes determine the relative concentrations of these isotopes within the groundwater from which the calcite eventually forms. So, isotope concentrations—notably those of the stable carbon-13 and oxygen-18—vary over time. The carbon levels relate to biological activity at the earth's surface and the oxygen is related to atmospheric factors such as temperature and precipitation. Both relationships are complex, but broad ideas about trends can be devised. A decline in carbon-13, for instance, is suggestive of an increase in biological activity within the soil zone, where carbonic acid and organic acids are created. In fact, the intensity and mode of photosynthesis is responsible for the falling signature. Oxygen-18 concentrations in the groundwater provide a direct reflection of the nature of the precipitation above the cave. Oxygen isotope levels are affected by cave temperature at the time of deposition, surface temperature, the path along which the storms have travelled to the cave and the composition of the ocean water source. In this region, on the

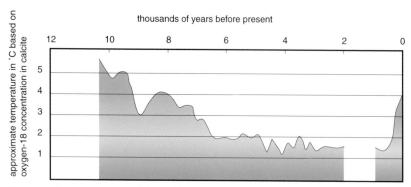

Figure 5.7. A temperature record derived from several Holocene stalagmites from Rat's Nest Cave. The temperature has been inferred from the oxygen-18 composition of calcite.

eastern side of the Rocky Mountains, a fall in the oxygen-18 composition is generally taken to indicate a fall in average temperature above the cave (around 2°C present day).

So what do we have? When we put all of our Holocene speleothem results together, we find the oxygen-18 level on average fell from about 10,000 years to 4500 years ago, when its decrease levelled out (with significant fluctuations) through to around 500 years ago (ignoring a 1000 year gap in the record!). This implies a temperature fall of around 4°C, but we must understand that the temperature is inferred from the isotope record, which is itself made up of a variety of components. Thereafter, the temperature seems to rise a couple of degrees to the present day (Figure 5.7). Overall, this suggests that temperature rose quickly at the end of the intense late Wisconsin glaciation, only to fall later. Interestingly, logs preserved in alpine meadows and bogs show that between 9500 and 5200 years ago tree line was up to 100 m higher than it is today in the Canadian Rockies. In fact, there are two well-known episodes of global warming during this period, known as hypsithermals. Our records indicate at least one significant warming pulse at around 8000 years BP. There is, however, a gap of about a thousand years or less at the beginning of our Holocene record. This was an interesting time, for we know that about 11,000 years ago native peoples inhabited the shores of Vermilion Lake near Banff. There is also a general worldwide interest in the global climate at this time, which is named the Younger Dryas, after a region in Europe. During this period, toward the end of the last glaciation, the climate became warmer very rapidly, only to cool again between 11,000 and 10,000 years ago (at the end of which the Rat's Nest speleothems start to grow). In the Canadian Rockies its effects manifested in the re-advance of the Crowfoot Glacier up to the present position of the Icefields Parkway.

It is this rapid change from glacial to interglacial and back to glacial conditions that has captured the interest of climatologists worldwide. In Canada, for example, there were two glacial advances during this time (the Peyto Glacier and later the Cavell Glacier, the latter equivalent to the

European Little Ice Age), so the climatologists wonder just how quickly a new ice age could descend upon us. In any event, the cooling, levelling out and final warming that is seen in the Rat's Nest Cave record may be important. The final warming starting around 500 years ago exhibited by our records may be natural. Add to this the effects of anthropological global warming and a very sharp climb in temperatures worldwide might be in the cards. Indeed, we have seen a rapid retreat of glaciers in the Rocky Mountains over the last 150 years, and the story is similar in other areas.

The most recent part of the Rat's Nest Cave record comes from W2, a diminutive stalagmite composed of translucent white calcite a few centimetres tall. We have also done some fairly detailed optical luminescence work on this deposit, and as stated above, the density of luminescence relates to solar intensity and can vary with sunspot cycles. During the final rise in temperature we also see a rise in optical density implying increased biological activity in this period (the same luminescence record is seen in a speleothem from a cave in Iowa). When we look at the sunspot activity, we see that it was intense from 2000 to 1700 years before the present, so there is probably some relationship between the intensity of sunspot activity and the later recovery in temperature. Recently, a link has been recognized between the weather and the sun's tendency to distort the shape of the earth's magnetic field.

During my organized cave tours I invariably demonstrate luminescence in the cave by holding a light against the calcite formations, then rapidly moving it away and turning it off. As the lurid green glow from the calcite dies away I am always intrigued by the thought that here, deep inside the cave, we are observing a phenomenon that tells us about the sun's past history. And all the while the sun is shining happily (sometimes!) onto the earth's surface way above us.

Yavor Shopov, a Bulgarian, first developed the techniques to investigate luminescence in cave deposits while working at the University of Sophia. Later Yavor refined his methods, working first with Derek Ford at McMaster University, and then with me at the University of Calgary. Eventually, he was able to resolve luminescent intensities under the microscope, as layers in the speleothems. In some cases the structure was so fine as to define annual events rather than the layers we can easily see. As already mentioned, the layers normally observed in sectioned speleothems represent hundreds or thousands of years, so Yavor's work added a new dimension to the resolution and precision of speleothem climate studies. In 1996 it was extremely gratifying to see Yavor and the importance of his work recognized at a scientific conference in Norway, and those luminescent layers are now referred to as Shopov Bands.

6 Cave and the Modern Environment

We have described the cave's geological history insofar as we understand it, from the tropical days of the lower Carboniferous when the cave rock was being laid down as primitive coral reefs to the here and now. But how is the cave today? Later we talk about cave life, a discipline known as speleobiology, and the chemical environment and mineralogy, but here we look at the current physical situation. Where does the cave go inside Grotto Mountain and how does that relate to its current climate? How do we go about recording the cave for posterity, mapping it, photographing it and so on?

The Cave Temperature and Humidity

Occasionally, if rarely, the summer weather in the Canadian Rockies gets very hot (up to +35°C). On such days I have had visitors call up wanting to go underground and cool off! Conversely, the winters can be arctic (the adjacent prairies have a Siberian climate) with temperatures falling to -35°C or lower. Skiers call up claiming it is too cold to ski and want to sample the balmy +5°C in the cave. On these occasions the cave feels as if it has central heating. Indeed, approaching the cave on very cold days you see steam rising from the entrance up the canyon wall. A spectacular ice rime develops there as vapour is frozen out from the moist cave air mass. We have analyzed the ice isotopically to confirm that it is cave water vapour that is being distilled as it rises and freezes on the face. We find that the isotopically heavier species of oxygen (^{18}O) and hydrogen (deuterium) get frozen out first—a process known as Rayleigh distillation. Such results help us to understand how permanent ice in other Albertan caves is formed—but that's another story.

The rising steam indicates just how moist the cave air is. In fact, we have found that only a few metres inside the cave the humidity reaches 100 per cent and condensed water droplets glint crystal-like from the cave ceiling. The humidity provides temporary relief if you suffer from asthma or have a cold—unfortunately, the symptoms return once you leave the cave. In Hungary, I visited a cave that served as a hospice for patients with lung ailments. Hospital beds were arranged in a large chamber. The resident doctors claimed that stays of several days cured many a malaise, saying that humidity and ionization from radioactive radon gas were the main benefits (radon is discussed later).

Humidity is good for the health of a cave. When a cave starts to dry out, the mineral formations lose their lustre; cave biota—liking the moist

Looking out of the cave entrance in winter. Hoarfrost has frozen out from warm air exiting the cave. Note ice stalagmites. Photo Ian Drummond.

environment—may also suffer. For arcane reasons I won't go into here, maintenance of 100 per cent humidity during mineral growth is important for our isotopic climate studies—evaporation processes can lead to an incorrect interpretation of the isotope signatures implanted as a result of climate variables.

Like humidity, the temperature also reaches a constant within a short distance of the cave entrance, +4.5°C (+40.1°F), to be precise. The constant temperature arises because of the huge thermal buffering of the surrounding rock. The rock is like a thick blanket over the cave. If the temperature changes at all, it does so over periods of hundreds of years, an important factor in our climate studies. For example, as the climate descends into a glacial regime, the cave temperature will slowly fall. Cave temperatures have been studied at a cave laboratory near Moulisse in France. Here, they measure temperature to 1/100 of a degree Celsius. Their conclusion is that minute fluctuations in temperature measured at depths of, say, 1.5 km below ground would be owing to climate effects 40,000 years ago; such is the thermal buffering power of the rock.

It is generally accepted that caves average out the surface temperatures—another important factor in our climate studies. This tends to be true in temperate and tropical caves, but in Rockies' caves this does not hold. The mean annual temperature for nearby Canmore is around 2.5°C, 2°C below that of the cave. At Castleguard Cave, Canada's longest running cave under the Columbia Icefield, the mean outside temperature is -10°C, whereas deep inside the 20 km-long cave system temperatures climb to +3°C. Why? The answer appears to be that in the cooler regions, geothermal heating is sufficient to manifest itself in the caves.

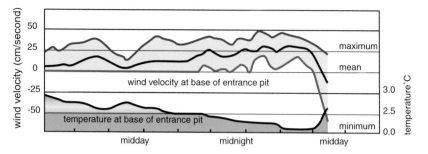

Figure 6.1. Maximum and minimum wind velocity and temperature over 34 hours at the constriction of the base of the Bone Bed. The recorder started at 4:00 am, December 23, ending at 2:00 pm, December 24, 1988.

Cave Winds

On our tours, visitors often remark on the fresh air they are breathing. There is an expectation that cave air may be bad in some way. Although there are caves where this is the case—for example, some tropical caves can be high in methane and carbon dioxide, where rotting vegetation has been flushed into them—most caves have very good air circulation. In Rat's Nest Cave the air is fresh and occasionally we experience strong drafts, especially where the cave narrows. The drafts can give you information about the cave, and we are always drawn to digs in the cave from which air is blowing. The Birth Canal was such an excavation and led to 2 km of uncharted passage beyond (see the chapter on exploration). The way in which drafts blow can point to any one of the following factors: the cave could have another entrance; it may be a response to pressure changes outside; there could be a temperature difference between inside and out; or the cave could oscillate in response to winds outside (much as you blow over the top of a bottle to produce a tone). The reason can be complex and involve some or all of these things.

In December of 1988, we set up a monitoring station for temperature, humidity and wind velocity at the base of the Bone Bed in the squeeze where the draft is usually strong. We managed 34 hours of data before casual visitors disturbed it (the anemometer propeller got jammed against the wall). We have already talked about temperature and humidity, but what of the airflow?

The airflow is outward most of the time, although it reverses at the end of the period. In winter so-called chimney winds commonly operate in caves. The inside air, being warmer than the outside, rises out of the entrance, drawing in cool air that becomes warmed by the surrounding rock and moistened by the damp cave environment. In summer we encounter the reverse when the cave air sinks and the warmer outside air is drawn in. The "sinking" process requires a lower entrance, and this we have yet to discover. However, at the base of the valley we have both springs and one mysterious area near the car park where the gravel "breathes." The reversal of airflow at the end of the record is oscillatory—the cave is both breathing in and out within an hourly period (the averaging period for our monitoring station). This phenomenon could be because of the "bottle effect" when air is blown across a bottle mouth producing a low sound. The standing waves so produced move air in and out cyclically. Winds may have been strong after midday on this day before Christmas—possibly a warm chinook wind associated with the rising temperature, which we had also monitored.

We observe two cycles in the airflow record: two hours and 24 hours. The latter cycle we expected, because it is observed regularly in caves, marking differences in the day (lower velocity) and night (higher velocity) temperatures. The higher velocities, for example, would be associated with an enhanced winter chimney effect during the cooler nights.

The two-hour fluctuation may also be owing to the bottle effect, but operating from deeper reaches in the cave. (High winds across the entrance might produce a standing wave to the first constriction, whereas lower winds might allow the cave to respond beyond those constrictions.) In any event, we can make a calculation regarding the size of the cave assuming it acts as a simple Helmholz resonator, a calculation that works for bottles!

$$l = 5.26T\sqrt{S}/_A$$

Where l is the length of the passage, T is the breathing cycle in seconds, S is the cross-sectional area of the neck-like breathing passage and A is the average cross-sectional area of the cave. All length dimensions are in metres.

For the passage at the base of the Bone Bed where the anemometer was set up, $T = 2$ hours, $S = 0.1$ m^2 and $A = 10$ m^2, which gives a cave length of 38 km, the theoretical length of the cave based on likely drainage routes! In fact, we know the cave to be complex—not only are narrow tubes connected to large chambers, there are parallel routes also. A more appropriate mathematical model would be the complex Helmholtz resonator. In general, such a resonator would have a longer period and this is what our calculation suggests. For example, if we reduce the period by a factor of 10—not unreasonable considering the complexities of Rat's Nest Cave—we obtain a figure of 4.7 km, which is roughly equivalent to the 4 km mapped presently. A less than hourly averaging might reveal shorter period fluctuations. In any event, natural systems are usually very complex and while it is fun to play these physics games, we can really only get a vague idea of what is going on. However, speculation can spur the caver to find something new, although it's amazing how often one is wrong and the cave does something quite unexpected.

Radon in the Cave Air: Radon and the Cave's Atmosphere

Radon has been very much in the news lately where attention has focussed mainly on buildings (1500 deaths annually are attributed to radon in Britain, for example). However, how radon behaves is not fully understood, and caves serve as controlled environments where it may be studied (essentially constant temperature, humidity and air movement). But studies have now been extended to monitor the threat of radon to cavers, and this is, of course, relevant for those of us that guide in Rat's Nest Cave regularly. For visitors who only visit the cave once or twice, it is much less of a problem.

Radon is the product of 238-uranium decay, arising after a series of decays, which yield radioactive "daughters" via α- and ß-particle emissions. Radon is doubly dangerous because it has a short half-life of around four days and appears in the cave atmosphere as a gas that can be breathed in. Uranium is either in the bedrock itself, in the cave sediments or is dissolved in the groundwater. From groundwater, it can subsequently be precipitated out in the various mineral formations.

Radon decays to give the short-lived lead isotopes, polonium and bismuth, damaging α-particles. Radon itself decays to give beta radiation in addition to α-particles. When ingested, either in the air, on dust particles or on water droplets, radon decays in the body causing serious cell damage that can lead to lung cancer.

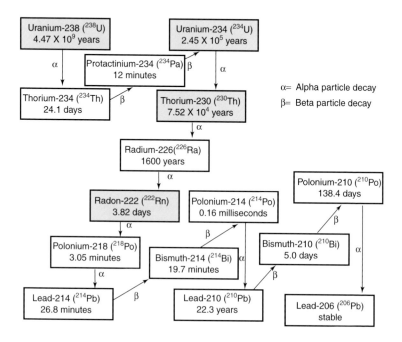

Figure 6.2. Uranium 238 decay scheme that features radon gas and ^{230}Th, the latter useful with ^{234}U for aging data.

Reading the compass while mapping the cave. Photo Dave Thomson.

Dr. Ann-Lise Norman (an undergraduate at the time of study) and Professor John Bland, both from the Department of Physics and Astronomy at the University of Calgary, made the radon measurements. They collected radon by absorbing it onto activated charcoal placed in canisters. After analysis, they obtained a value of 1.87 working levels (WL). Working levels are a measure of the radiation dose received relative to recommended maximum exposure time. In assessing the risk to health it is necessary to compute dose or working level hours (WLH), and 204 WLH per year is considered safe.

At Rat's Nest Cave only 109 hours (204 WLH divided by 1.87 WL) underground in any one year would be allowed—about 30 trips a year for the guides. We are assured, however, that the high humidity in the cave, which is readily absorbed into activated charcoal, will give this figure as an absolute maximum. In addition, radon concentrations vary wildly in space and time. Needless to say, we will continue monitoring as it affects our personal safety. In any event, we know our visitors are a long way from being at risk on a three-four hour tour.

The Cave Map: Where Does the Cave Go?

If you peruse the detailed cave map reproduced in this book, you will find 15 names on it. These 15 individuals have spent hours and hours in the cave mapping the passage complex. The result: more than 4 km of passageways logged. How did we do this?

First, we need to find direction and a compass serves this purpose. Second, we want to find out whether the cave is going up or down, so we use a clinometer, which gives us positive angles when it is pointed up a slope and negative ones for the down directions. Third, a tape measure made of nonstretching fibron provides the distance between stations. The compass and clinometer we used are hand-held devices. You sight them onto some point in the passage (rock, projection or some other feature), peer through a lens aperture and read off the numbers. Surprisingly, such instruments can give you an accuracy of around one per cent. The surveyors' conversation might go like this:

"On station!" says the person with the tape measure, who then highlights

Rat's Nest Cave (Bone Bed to duck)
August 10, 1988

Station	Tape	Compass	Climo	Vert	Horiz
18				0.3	5.0
	5.50	005	+45		
19				0.3	3.5
	4.30	016	+08		
20				0.3	1.5
	8.00	329	+25		
21				1.0	3.0
	5.66	311	+12		
22				1.0	1.0
	7.33	304	⁻06		
23				1.0	3.0
	7.10	317	+12		
24				1.2	1.8
	5.90	258	⁻04		
25				1.5	2.5
	4.60	344	+14		
26				1.5	1.8

Figure 6.3. A typical page from a Rat's Nest Cave survey notebook.

the station feature with his or her light. The instrument person then sights to the feature from the previous station and reads the numbers. "Tape 8.15 m, compass 259°, clino -17°."

The book person then tabulates this data in a field book, while at the same time making an approximate sketch. I actually make a "guestimated" scale map using the compass directions and tape lengths so that any miscommunicated data immediately becomes apparent. For example, if I had heard 359° instead of 259° and then tried to sketch this incorrect direction, the sketch would not look right. While measurements are made

Reading the clinometer while mapping the cave. Photo Dave Thomson.

from station to station, it is up to the book person to flesh out the map by drawing rocks, formations, passage shapes and other notable features—that's where the blend of art, experience and science comes in. Additional measurements that aid the drawing are passage widths and heights, either measured or estimated, at each station. With these a plan and elevation of the cave can be drawn or a 3-D rendering produced. Passage cross-sections are also sketched whenever the cave changes shape—say from a tube to a rift passage.

Back at home, your computer processes the data—commercial cave-plot programs are available to do this, and I was ably assisted by Pierre Lebel of the ASS. Apart from giving you line plots of one sort or another, the program also processes passage loops. If I survey an oxbow passage that leads off from and comes back to a main lead, the inherent error in the instruments (one per cent) means the tie-in won't quite match up. The software will make small adjustments to each station to station leg so that the survey matches up. Loops are useful in making the survey self-checking, as it were.

Once the line plots are produced—a kind of wire diagram of the cave—you can flesh out the survey using your field notes. Having already made a rough map in the field book aids this process considerably. While computer software can allow you to produce a camera-ready map, in practice cave maps are complicated enough that it is often better to draft the maps by hand. At present, the association is drawing Canada's longest cave, Castleguard, which is 20 km long. We're wrestling with a 6 m-long piece of paper!

Confirming the Survey with the Cave Radio

"We'll move on to the Terminus and transmit again at 13:30, over and out," says a crackling voice through 150 m of limestone. The surface party folds up the loop antenna, closes the metallic suitcases containing the radio and prepares to move on.

Ian Drummond (whose photographs you will see in this book) is not only an accomplished cave photographer, but is also talented in electronics. He has built a series of cave radios based on designs by cave radio enthusiasts worldwide. We used Ian's radio at Rat's Nest Cave, going to the far reaches of the system to check the cave's position with respect to the land surface. This provides an independent check on the survey. All of the survey data is based on measurements made from the only entrance to the cave. As you proceed through the cave from your entrance datum, systematic errors build up; the cave radio puts you back on track.

How? At a prearranged time and place, the underground party sets up a loop antenna; the coil being laid horizontally. The loop (and radio) transmits 200-300 m-long radio waves to the surface unit. Initially the surface party uses voice transmission, and as it nears the location, they switch to a beacon pulse tone. Then the nitty-gritty: finding the actual depth and location of the beacon. The underground, horizontal loop sends out an alternating electromagnetic field, the shape of which is similar to a magnetic field from a bar magnet standing on end. The field lines of force travel out of the land surface and the surface antenna receives and tracks them. As the mathematical equations for the field lines are well known, surface points on the lines can be related to the lines' source—the underground loop. Thus depth and position can be calculated.

When we did this the first time at Rat's Nest Cave, I opted to be in the surface party thinking it would be pleasant to wander about with the radio in the sunshine on a nice summer day. Well, the nice summer day turned into a blizzard with us trying to talk to the underground party with windblown sleet travelling horizontally past our vision. We did get results at the Terminus and the High Point, but the results were inconclusive. The second time we tried was in January on a reasonably warm day under sunny skies. We got good results at four locations ending finally at the High Point. There, high up on the ridge to the west of the cave canyon, the overburden is around 160 m. The results have determined that the cave map is off only by a degree or so and it is clear that the cave is heading into the heart of Grotto Mountain (see Figure 6.4). We now know that there must be a substantial amount of cave we have yet to discover, as the cave should traverse to the far side of the mountain.

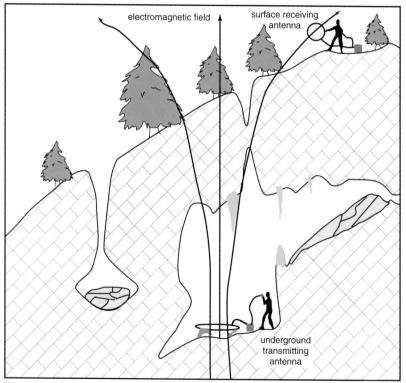

Figure 6.4. Schematic showing the use of the cave radio. Depth of position underground can be determined by radio location.

The Grotto with extensive flowstone formation. Photo Ian Drummond.

Draperies in the Grotto. Photo Tom Barton.

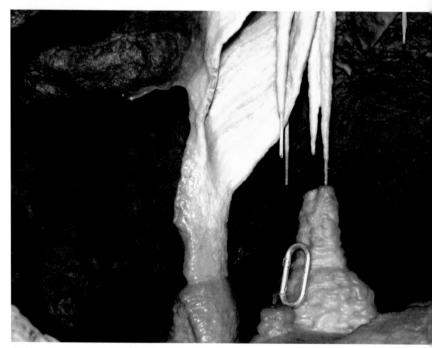

Column formation with carabiner for scale. Photo Tom Barton.

Massive flowstone in the Grotto. Photo Tom Barton.

Stalagmites, stalactites and curtain formations beyond the Birth Canal. Photo Dave Thomson.

Author viewing the Wedding Cake stalagmite. Photo Dave Thomson.

Dr. James Burns views a black bear skull at the Bone Bed. Other skulls are bighorn sheep.

Column, Wedding Cake Passage. Photo Dave Thomson.

Surveying carefully among cave formations in the new section. Photo Dave Thomson.

Surveying above the Slimy Climb. The passage is developed along a fault line. Photo Dave Thomson.

Descending the 18 m pitch on the Adventure Tour. Photo Dave Thomson.

7 Mineral Formations

We invariably find mineral calcite deposited in the cave. This is not too surprising as the cave is formed in very pure limestone (the Livingstone and Mount Head formation), which itself is composed predominantly of calcite ($CaCO_3$).

Groundwater seeping downward from the surface, especially if it comes from the biologically active soil zone, is charged with carbon dioxide. The soil CO_2 has a high partial pressure (pCO_2) and it is dissolved in the groundwater forming carbonic acid. The acid attacks the underlying limestone, but becomes neutralized as it travels through the bedrock via cracks, joints and fissures. On emerging into a cave, the groundwater meets an atmosphere with a low pCO_2 and it therefore loses its CO_2 to the cave air. As it does so, the groundwater can no longer hold its dissolved load and it precipitates calcite, giving us the wonderful display of mineral formations that we associate with caves. This mechanism accounts for most of the mineral formations (called speleothems) we see in caves. Occasionally, evaporation of the seeping water can produce similar results, but it is far less than is usually thought as cave air usually has humidity close to 100 per cent.

Calcite mineral formation at the Grotto. Photo Ian Drummond.

There are other mechanisms, too. For example, if the surface is colder than the cave, then groundwater can, against intuition, dissolve more CO_2 than it would underground. The effect is that mineral-charged waters entering the cave become warmed (relatively), and CO_2 is lost to the cave and precipitation of calcite takes place. While we do not see speleothems being formed during full glacial times, this phenomenon can account for the growth of mineral deposits during colder periods, especially if there is no soil cover. For example, some speleothems in Castleguard Cave, which runs right under the Columbia Icefield, may have formed from CO_2-charged water from the base of the glacial ice.

In any event, we can write a simple chemical reaction for the dissolving of limestone and the subsequent re-precipitation of calcite in caves.

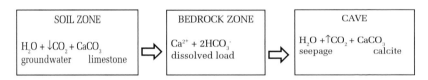

SOIL ZONE	BEDROCK ZONE	CAVE
$H_2O + \downarrow CO_2 + CaCO_3$ groundwater limestone	$Ca^{2+} + 2HCO_3^-$ dissolved load	$H_2O + \uparrow CO_2 + CaCO_3$ seepage calcite

The CO_2 in the H_2O forms carbonic acid (H_2CO_3), which acts on the limestone ($CaCO_3$) to produce the "dissolved load" seen in the middle of the equation.

Speleothems are found in a huge variety of shapes and sizes, controlled by factors such as water flow, gravity and so on. Throughout the 4 km-long length of Rat's Nest Cave we find such a range of deposits, complemented here with photographs. Stalagmites and stalactites occur as primary deposits from dripping water where they are elongated in the vertical direction. Flowing water generates flowstone and rimstone dams. Coralloids and sparry calcite grow underwater in mineral saturated pools. Helictites twist in all directions as water seeps from microscopic, internal canals. Calcite rafts form on the surface of pools, supported initially by surface tension. Cave pearls form when particles such as sand grains are tossed around by water dripping into puddles.

Soda straw with helictite.
Photo Dave Thomson.

Combination stalactite-stalagmite formation with soda straws. Photo Dave Thomson.

Speleothem colouring can vary from white to creamy to honey coloured and even to black. Generally, we see a variation in colour, exhibited beautifully in the curtain formations where a banded, streaky-bacon texture is apparent. The colour, as Mel Gascoyne (a graduate from the cave and karst study group at McMaster University) discovered, was as a result of very small quantities of organics combined with the optical properties of calcite in the main. Organics, for example, can lead to the aesthetically-pleasing deep honey-coloured appearance of stalagmites. Minute concentrations of trace metals can also lead to coloured speleothems.

Below I have listed the various speleothem forms found in the cave in alphabetical order. For those of you who have, or will, visit the cave this list should be a useful reference.

Coatings and Crusts
These are perhaps the least spectacular but most common speleothems seen. They are the light-coloured mineral patina lining the walls and floors, where they form a base for subsequent, more spectacular speleothem growth. We see calcite coating thick deposits of mud as at the Birth Canal and above the Slimy Climb. The coating in both circumstances has been very useful to our dating program as we can determine when the mud stopped accumulating (see Chapter 5 describing Ancient Environments). One other significant feature of crusting has been to provide a substrate for the growth of helictites.

Conulites

Until the Birth Canal was excavated in the late 1980s, conulites had not been reported. This may well have been because unknowing visitors trampled them underfoot in the mud. Often not seen, conulites—sometimes called vases or mud cups—are conical shells of calcite, which form a downward apex in the mud floor. When drips fall a long way, they excavate the mud and coat the resulting cavity with calcite. Sometimes delicate vases form when the mud is washed from the outside. Rat's Nest Cave possesses ideal sites for conulites as it is floored with fine glacial mud and has high ceilings up to 40 m. The chasm below the High Point chamber has excellent conulites of the "bird-bath" variety. The long fall of drips causes a flattening and convoluting of the more typical conical form, and some have diameters of up to 20 cm.

Coralloids

This is an all-embracing term describing a variety of nodular, globular, botryoidal and coral-like speleothems. In the cave, both subaerial and underwater varieties can be seen. Of the first kind only "popcorn" exists, which is owing mainly to evaporation. The entrance is one of the best places to see it. It forms from drip water, but unlike other deposits, water oozes out from the wall and the component crystals rather than through capillaries. Of the second kind, numerous examples can be seen in standing pools and pools behind rimstone dams, which tend to be saturated in calcite. Mostly the appearance is that of cauliflower clinging to the walls and floor of pools and marks a prominent calcite rim at the water line—clearly seen when pool levels drop. The mechanism of formation is the same

Calcite filaments growing downward underwater from a calcite raft. Photo Dave Thomson.

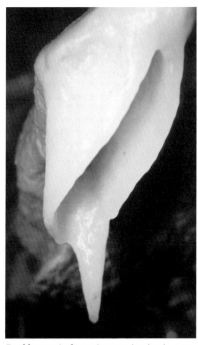

as described above, where carbon dioxide slowly bubbles from the pool and calcite is precipitated. The Grotto, visited on the regular tour, has excellent examples.

We have found some very unusual needle-like forms in the Mud Room. Here these needles have grown in parallel upright arrays sandwiched between two calcite slabs. These slabs have their origin in rafts (described later), which formed at earlier water level stages in the pool.

Curtains

The cave has fine examples of these deposits. This is because the cave has developed along an inclined fault, which allows drip water to run down the ceilings and walls under surface tension. As the drip proceeds, it leaves a trail of calcite before it eventually falls away to the floor. Where it breaks away a stalactite forms. Eventually the cal-

Double curtain formation terminating in a stalactite. Photo Dave Thomson.

Curtain formation with carrots on left. Photo Dave Thomson.

cite trail builds to a thin curtain (or drapery), giving it a characteristic "bacon-slice" texture owing to the variation of trace elements in the water over time. Excellent examples can be viewed on our tour in the Grand Gallery, or less accessibly, in Coyote Descent where the ceiling is steeply inclined.

Flowstone

This is a very common form resembling a frozen waterfall. It is the most common speleothem found in the cave for similar reasons that curtains are common. Whereas the ceiling is steeply inclined giving draperies, so the sloping walls and floor give flowstone. It occurs where water flows in thin films over surfaces, the increased surface area of water allows the greater escape of carbon dioxide, resulting in calcite being precipitated. In the cave there

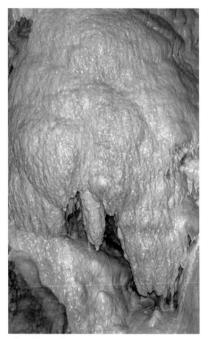

Flowstone. Photo Tom Barton.

have been periods when sluggish, mineral-saturated streams have flowed down passageways such as in the Wedding Cake (the Frozen River). Here flowstone (along with rimstone dams) has formed over tens of metres. In some cases the cave is completely floored with flowstone, especially where passages follow the dip direction of the rock as at the start of the Wedding Cake Passage.

Flowstone yields good material for dating and paleoenvironmental studies, as it tends to form in layers that can be followed for some distance, which permits detailed investigation.

Helictites. Photo Dave Thomson.

Helictites

A helictite is a speleothem that twists and turns unexpectedly in any direction. In 1886, Dolly first coined the term, which comes from the Greek "to spiral." Helictites grow on walls, ceilings and other speleothems; in Rat's Nest Cave they are frequently seen growing from crusts. They are best viewed in a dazzling display in the first chamber beyond the Birth Canal, but can also be seen at the Grotto as part of the cave tour. In the cave, helictites are of the filiform (threadlike) variety less than 1 mm in diameter.

Stalagmite. Photo Dave Thomson.

Helictites have in common tiny central canals through which nutrients feed their extremities. A number of theories have been proposed for their apparently random morphology. The current one involves a primary mechanism of hydrostatic pressure and capillary action combined with secondary processes such as evaporation, airflow, impurities in solution, water supply and intercrystalline seepage. A porous rock face, usually encrusted with calcite, appears to be necessary for the initiation of helictite growth. Branching of helictites may occur where there is a blockage in the central canal, which forces the water out sideways to generate a new limb.

Curiously, in Rat's Nest a number of helictites terminate in hollow, parallel stalactites called soda straws. It may be that as the helictite ages its central channel becomes enlarged by resolution, enhancing water supply to its tip. The water dripping out then forms a stalactite under gravity. (Why soda straws are hollow is explained later under stalactites.) Another possibility is that while the helictite is growing close to the cave wall, it is subject to turbulent drafts, which make it grow in random directions. When farther from the wall, airflow becomes more laminar and gravity can take over. Perhaps here is an example in nature where a chaotic attractor changes at a threshold to become a single-point attractor!

Moonmilk

This is a speleothem, which in some circumstances may have its origins in life. Therefore, moonmilk as a living organism can be found in the chapter on cave life. Here we look at chemical origins. Texture, not composition, is implied by the term moonmilk. It is soft, plastic and pasty when wet (its healthy state), but becomes powdery when dry. In its normal state it can contain up to 40-70 per cent water. Three theories on the chemical origin (and one on the biological origin) seem to have been accepted from the

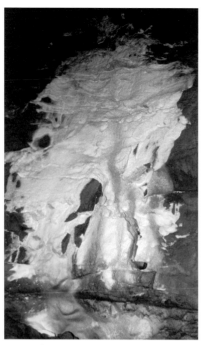

Moonmilk at the 18 m pitch.
Photo Dave Thomson.

surprising plethora of literature on the subject. Two of these, that of freezing seepage water just within the cave wall and the disintegration of bedrock with corrosive fluids, seem unlikely for Rat's Nest. First, the cave remains at 5°C year round and does not freeze. And second, breakdown occurs in massive ancient fragments that probably fell down under stress when the cave was drained at the end of one or other glacial period. Corrosive fluids, which would cause more localized breakdown, are not in evidence.

Therefore, for Rat's Nest moonmilk is either biological in origin or has formed according to the third theory. This theory, which is one most accepted by speleologists, is that moonmilk is directly precipitated from groundwater, as are other calcite minerals, but for some reason the crystals never become large. Why they do not form in a more normal way is a puzzle yet to be solved. Scanning electron micrographs reveal crystal sizes of a few microns (1 micron = 1/1000th of a mm), whereas stalagmites, for example, can contain calcite crystals centimetres across. Incidentally, SEM images while showing micron-sized crystals occasionally exhibit organic filaments associated with them. Therefore, some moonmilk is undoubtedly of biological origin.

We find moonmilk beautifully displayed on the far wall of the first pitch barely 50 m from the entrance, where it covers the wall in a white blanket. Here we think it may well have biological origins. Deeper in the cave, as in the lower loop of the Wedding Cake Passage, moonmilk flowers may be of chemical (abiotic) origin.

Pearls

Cave pearls form as concentrically banded concretions in shallow pools. When cut they have an onion-like appearance. Usually, and this is the case in the cave, they are spherical, but they can be cylindrical, irregular or rarely, cubical (as in Castleguard Cave under the Columbia Icefield). Pearls were unknown in the cave until the Birth Canal was opened up and a number of nests were found in the Pearly Way as well as other locations—one having now been found in Ranger Way. Rat's Nest Cave pearls range in diameter from 1-10 mm, with large populations occurring in the smaller range. They occur where there is drip or flushing water that agitates sand grains, which form pearl nuclei. Once the pearl gets started, it accumulates layers of calcite as it is rolled around. As the pearls grow and the nests become constricted, the pearls may weld together or be agitated with limited freedom. It's the latter case that appears to account for cubic pearls.

Rafts

Sometimes referred to as cave ice, rafts are sheets of calcite that initially "float" on the surface of pools by surface tension. As you can imagine, the cave environment must be absolutely undisturbed for this to occur. In time, and before they thicken and sink, some of these rafts become anchored to the walls where they can continue to thicken. I was in a cave in England where we crawled along a wall to wall raft now marooned as the water had long disappeared. A deep, hollow and regular thump-thump emitting from the passage was inexplicable until I realized it was my heartbeat ampli-

Cave pearls in the Pearly Way.
Photo Dave Thomson.

fied by the drum-like sheet of calcite. Rat's Nest Cave has yielded only a few sightings of cave rafts, one in the Sucker Route (that difficult and constricted passage had to be good for something!) and one in the Mud Room that supports downward projecting needles. Other rafts may well have existed but have long since been trampled underfoot.

Rimstone Dams

These are barriers of calcite that obstruct cave streams or shallow flowing pools (sinter or gour dams are other terms in usage). In the Grotto there are superb examples in miniature, like terraced rice paddies viewed from the air. The rimstone terraces have formed as the top surface of flowstone. Many a visitor to the Grotto has mentioned that water falling down the flowstone does so in pulses. I think these pulses may initiate the dams. The accepted view is that the dams form at shallow points in flowing water. Where it is shallow the water film is thinner and carbon dioxide is lost there thus enhancing calcite precipitation at that point. Once the process is started it will be self-perpetuating. Rimstone dams can be found outside at hot springs. Essentially the same mechanism operates except that it is evaporation rather than the liberation of carbon dioxide that causes precipitation of the minerals.

The Frozen River in the Wedding Cake Passage contains the largest dams, which are startlingly white. Tragically, sections of these dams have been muddied and broken by careless feet over the last few years.

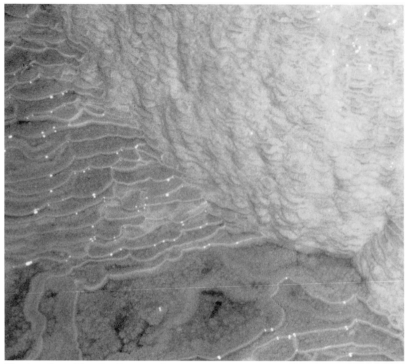

Rimstone dams. Photo Ian Drummond.

Spar

The term spar is reserved for mineral deposits where individual crystals are readily observable by eye. Spars are often unusual forms of calcite crystals looking like other types of minerals and hence are referred to as pseudomorphs. Nailhead and dogtooth spar are such examples and these can be seen in a number of places in the cave where pools have drained out. One such temporary pool is above the Slimy Climb where the passage suddenly gets lower—you are forced to crawl slightly painfully across nailhead spar. Here crystals form a mat across the floor as nails might be hammered closely into wood.

Stalactites

These are found throughout the cave growing from joints in the ceiling or from the margins of ledges. All stages of development are represented from narrow, parallel-sided soda straws to great calcite pendants, some of which have met their opposite number, stalagmites, to form massive columns.

In Rat's Nest Cave, stalactites almost invariably start life as soda straws or tubular stalactites (embryonic stalactites) and even massive stalactites when sectioned have the characteristic tubular channel within their cores. Water droplets, prior to falling to the floor, leave a trace of calcite on the surface from which they hang. This trace, which builds as successive drops fall, is circular since precipitation takes place around the rim of the drop. Eventually a straw is formed with water running down through its central channel. In the cave there are "clouds" of soda straws up to 30 cm long and typically with a diameter of about 5 mm. We have determined it takes around 2000 years at Rat's Nest to reach this length. The Grotto is an excellent location to view this phenomenon. Fragile as these formations are—a single careless touch will snap them off—blasting in the quarry about a kilometre away has not resulted in any breakage. Nonetheless, in the Wedding Cake Passage there is a population of 10 cm-long soda straws lying fallen and cemented on to a flowstone floor. Being cemented certainly precludes human breakage because of the length of time required for such a process to take place. What then: a massive earthquake that shook the cave in a way that blasting never could? Believe it or not, earthquakes do still occur in our area, if rarely, and giant ones probably occurred in the recent geological past.

Although soda straws can reach lengths of 3 m or so (as in Flabbergasm Chasm, Dan Yr Ogof Cave in Wales), something usually comes along to prevent this happening. Most often the channel becomes blocked with detritus. This forces the seeping water onto the outside and a "carrot" is formed. The carrot thickens out over time to form the more normal stalactite that we're all familiar with. As the stalactite advances downward it may eventually meet its partner stalagmite that is growing upward. Excellent examples of columns can be viewed in the Wedding Cake Passage. When stalactites grow downward from ledges or from the ends of curtains,

Flowstone terminating in a fringe of stalactites at a ledge. Photo Dave Thomson.

The Wedding Cake stalagmite.
Photo Dave Thomson.

Column with person for scale in the Wedding
Cake Passage. Photo Ian Drummond.

they do not generally start out as soda straws. A stalactite that had an interesting life of 200,000 years or so is 881010. Read about it in Chapter 5 on Ancient Environments.

Stalagmites

These are the stocky brethren of stalactites, formed from the same water droplet after it has fallen and splashed on the floor. The calcite dissolved in the droplet is not completely used up in forming a stalactite or, for that matter, a stalagmite. Only a small proportion of the dissolved load gets dumped in this process, around one per cent for Rat's Nest Cave although this is likely to be highly variable throughout the system. Some stalagmites are more than 15 cm in diameter and half a metre tall. Others, forming only very recently after the last glaciation, look like sand dollars or fried eggs lying atop muddy or sandy sediments.

The splashing action of the fallen droplet, and its subsequent flow outward, results in the stocky, parallel-sided appearance of stalagmites. In the Wedding Cake Passage there are splendid examples, pristine white and standing like soldiers. In other areas such as beyond the Slimy Climb there are yellow-brown stalagmites with a melted appearance. These are ancient deposits whose growth has been reversed by acidic groundwater dissolving their calcite fabric away; a chemical environment that can be prevalent during certain periods (for example, acidity can vary on a seasonal basis). Actually, we can see this re-solution phenomenon on many kinds of speleothems in Rat's Nest Cave. It probably occurs when large quantities

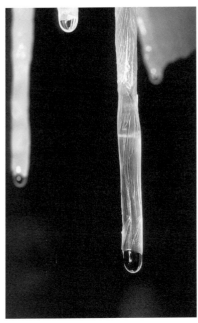

of seepage water are flushed through the bedrock. In this case, the contact with the bedrock is not enough to neutralize the acid. The yellow-brown "melted" stalagmites were redissolved in a slightly different way as they were inundated by floodwaters around 200,000 years ago. These "melted" stalagmites appear to be mates of stalactite 881010—read about this in Chapter 5 on Ancient Environments. To support the notion of cave flooding episodes, we have found other stalagmites in Ranger Way totally buried in fine sediments.

Detail of soda straw and drip. Photo Dave Thomson.

Soda straws in the new section of the cave. Photo Dave Thomson.

We find stalagmites with ages up to 730,000 years. There are probably older ones, but we are unable to date them because of the limits imposed by our dating methods. The longest period of growth we have found, although it's most unlikely to have been continuous, is from a large squat stalagmite found lying among breakdown (it was actually the smaller of a pair, but the larger one was stolen from the cave). Droplets had fallen, perhaps one every 10 seconds, building this formation for over 400,000 years.

TYPES OF CALCITE MINERAL FORMATION IN RAT'S NEST CAVE AND WHERE THEY ARE FOUND

Calcite Mineral Formation	Where Good Examples Are Found
Coatings and Crust	Birth Canal and above the Slimy Climb
Conulites	Chasm below the High Point, Grand Gallery
Coralloids	Grotto, Wedding Cake Passage, Rabbit Warren
Curtains	Grand Gallery, Coyote Descent
Flowstone	Many areas—Grotto, Great West Highway, Wedding Cake Passage
Helictites	Great West Highway, Wedding Cake Passage
Moonmilk	18 m pitch near entrance, high dome above the Grand Gallery
Pearls	Pearly Way, Ranger Way
Rafts	Sucker Route, Mud Room
Rimstone Dams	Frozen River in the Wedding Cake Passage, Grotto
Spar	Above the Slimy Climb
Stalactites	Numerous areas—Ranger Way, Great North Highway, Grand Gallery, Grotto
Stalagmites	Numerous areas—Ranger Way, Great North Highway, Grand Gallery, Grotto

8 Cave Life and the Bone Bed

The Living

Apart from the obvious presence of bushy-tailed wood rats, whose middens occupy ledges around the cave entrance, and occasional bats that flit by, other life in the cave is rather more elusive. It is tiny and requires a keen eye or a microscope to see it.

Stewart Peck, a biologist from Carleton University specializing in cave fauna, wrote that little is known of the fauna of Canadian caves. While he referred mainly to the study of microfauna, the same could be said of most of the life in Rat's Nest Cave. Apart from arachnid harvestmen or harvesters (daddy long-legs), the living biota had received scant attention. More recently, Heidi Macklin, a student from the University of Calgary, has studied the small fauna in the cave finding other arachnids, insects and earthworms. In addition, amateurs in the field of speleobiology have made a few observations while exploring and mapping the cave. In reference to the cave's biology, we should be comprehensive and include fungi and flora, although thus far we do not have much to say on either subject.

Of flora, there is almost nothing to report at present. Occasionally pack rats transport seeds inside the cave. These send out slender, ghost-like shoots, but deprived of sunlight, they soon fail. We know more about fungi. Let's imagine you are in the cave having a snack—a break in the midst of a tour, perhaps. A crumb falls to the floor even though you are being careful not to introduce foreign material into the cave. Then a day or so later on another trip you pass your meal stop and are intrigued to find a tiny forest of 2 cm-high silky-white fibres rising from the floor. Beneath this mat of fibres is your crumb covered with white fur. You also find that fresh pack rat droppings have undergone the same process. The fibres, or fungal mycelia, develop from spores carried in the relatively sterile cave air. They are the stalks of the fruiting bodies that grow from the spores, which latch onto any organic material available. Further observation reveals a piece of rotting wood apparently wrapped in a fine web-like lace. Fine, white filaments of fungi have grown out fan-like to embrace the morsel of timber. These fungi assist in breaking down organic material introduced into the cave. Old droppings, for example, are reduced to tiny piles of dust. The organic material is important in the cave's ecology forming the base of the food chain there, in which fungi play a part; indeed, Heidi has found fungus gnats living on this bounty.

Bushy-tailed wood rat in its midden surrounded by food it has collected from outside. Photo Ed Easterling.

A creamy white deposit covering the far wall of the 18 m pitch impressed the first explorers to the cave. In fact, visitors to the cave remark on it often as it is on the tour side of the cave. What they are observing is moonmilk. Moonmilk, translated from the German Mondmilch, is adulterated from monmilch, which means gnome's milk in German. In 15th century Switzerland, gnomes were thought to inhabit caves and such deposits were ascribed to them. While we're not sure in this case, moonmilk may be biologically derived from microorganismal activity. Species of bacteria, algae and fungi have all been isolated from it experimentally, but it seems that these are not essential factors in its formation. Moonmilk is made up of an aqueous form of calcite ($CaCO_3$) or of aragonite (the same composition but with a differing crystal structure). Unlike the usual stalagmite or stalactite calcite, moonmilk has a spongy texture like wet blotting paper, which tends to give the impression that it has biological origins. When viewed under a scanning electron microscope, some types of moonmilk can be seen as minute calcite rods surrounded by mineralized filaments. It is thought that the calcite grows (nucleates) along these filaments, which are composed of mold-like bacteria. This is something to think about while rappelling the pitch!

Next in order of increasing size is the microfauna—organisms individually visible to the eye if hard to spot. Interestingly, microfauna can evolve within a cave system quite quickly where they become cave-adapted. In the total darkness of the cave they can lose their sight—although vestigial eyes remain—their colour, and so on. In North America, most cave-evolved species are found beyond the southern limit of the Pleistocene glacial ice sheet, which essentially means south of Canada. Covered by ice during a series of glaciations in the Quaternary, Rat's Nest Cave may well contain organisms that predate glacial events. Such organisms have been discovered happily living in pools in Castleguard Cave, Canada's longest cave that terminates right under the Columbia Icefield. In such a so-called glacial refugium, invertebrates may evolve divergently, independent of their counterparts on the surface. Unfortunately, apart from anecdotal reports, no invertebrates have been observed in the cave pools at Rat's Nest, although a careful observer might one day find colourless isopod worms or amphipods (minute shrimp-like organisms) as we do at Castleguard. I've looked often enough, but I don't have that special biologist's eye to see them.

What we do see are single-strand webs in moist areas of the cave. It is possible these webs have been spun by a tubular worm (such worms live in caves in the Ozark Mountains in the USA). Some of the webs have been sampled recently, and these contain something, but whether it is predator or prey we do not yet know. Tubular worms can make these single webs by turning themselves inside out, crawling through themselves, while spinning out a slimy thread. The threads then trap minute flies, which are consumed by the predatory worms. Heidi suggests the single-strand webs are most likely fungus gnat larvae, so my fanciful ideas about tubular worms may be rendered to the more commonplace!

We regularly see sinuous tracks crisscrossing clean-washed muddy floors, but never see what made them. It appears now that these tracks are made by the common earthworm.

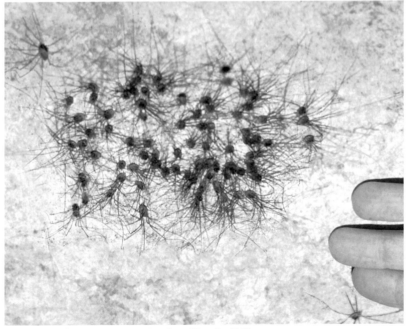

Overwintering harvesters in Rat's Nest Cave. Photo Jon Rollins.

Over the years we have observed life forms far into the cave. Winged insects, probably gnats, have been found in the Wedding Cake Passage cemented into flowstone, which suggests a certain antiquity, and a beetle has been found near the Hose-pipe Passage. Perhaps it is not surprising to find insects and their remains in Rat's Nest Cave as it never freezes, remaining at a constant 4.5°C. At the entrance, harvestmen, mosquitoes, gnats, crickets, beetles and other insects hibernate in the warm air that rises out of the cave. Harvestmen, commonly called daddy long-legs spiders, are technically opiliones—a type of arachnid related to spiders. In the first chamber of the cave, plate-sized clusters of harvestmen hang in vibrating masses from the walls in wintertime. If disturbed, these masses will break up and emit a strong odour from their scent glands as a defense mechanism. In fact, the combined odour of all the scent glands—over 1500 have been counted in a single cluster—would be decidedly repulsive to a potential predator.

The table on page 92 lists the common names for the orders and families only, so the real diversity of fauna in Rat's Nest Cave is bigger than this. Heidi notes the wingless crane fly and grylloblattids (ice-crawler) are exceptionally rare insects that are found only at high elevations or in caves at lower elevations. The ice-crawler—whose life cycle takes seven years—has as its primary food source the wingless crane fly, which is why they always hang out together.

Although Heidi's study did not find midges, they may have been observed on occasion. However, amateurs regularly mistake midges for gnats. They look superficially like mosquitoes, but those living in the Canadian Rocky Mountains do not bite. They like to occupy limestone openings in montane and subalpine areas and can be seen as compact swarms on summer evenings when they emerge.

Crickets are very common in caves especially in the USA where they can be numerous in the twilight zone of caves. In the rather cooler Rat's Nest Cave we see the odd one; small and dark, which may be the field cricket. These live in montane forest areas consuming seeds, fruits, young plants and dead insects. They usually die at the first heavy frost, having laid their eggs in the soil. The young emerge in spring. At sites like Rat's Nest Cave, which never freezes, some crickets survive over the winter.

There are around 3000 species of beetles in North America, and three appear to inhabit the cave; these are the rove beetle, the scarab beetle and the feathery wing beetle (the smallest-sized beetle). Beetles like moist zones under rocks and soil—and apparently the interior of caves where they can be found far underground.

Bats are seen occasionally flying through the cave. The most common sightings have occurred in the passage complex at the end of the Great West Highway, in Coyote Descent and the Ranger Way. A bat skull in the Wedding Cake Passage and other remains confirm that some of these individuals are little brown bats. One sick little brown bat was retrieved and identified by Chris Butler, a ranger from Bow Valley Provincial Park. There may also be big brown bats as these too are common in southern Alberta and like to roost in caves. A silver-haired bat has been identified in the Bone Bed.

Little brown bats in Wapiabi Cave, Eastern Slopes. Photo Dave Thomson.

These occasional sightings of bats suggest to us that a substantial roost must exist in some hitherto undiscovered part of the cave. For example, farther north on the Eastern Slopes in Alberta, Cadomin Cave contains a large bat population. Caves close to Jasper in the Athabasca River valley also contain bats, but the populations are smaller, except at Disaster Point Cave, which contains a veritable graveyard of bat skeletons from a now defunct population. One surprising fact is little brown bats can live for up to 30 years. Jasper naturalist Ben Gadd reports seeing banded bats over a period of many years at Cadomin Cave. When we come across bats hibernating in caves, we are very careful not to disturb them. In the torpid state their body temperature is very low and energy consumption minimal. Their body temperature can drop by as much as 30°C (to around 7°C) and they may breath only once every three minutes. If woken and agitated, the increased demand on their energy reserves may mean they will not survive the winter—body weight can drop by one-third over the hibernation period. Bats are delightful creatures and need friends; just think of those pesky mosquitoes and deer flies, which would be far more numerous if bats weren't around. In numbers, bats represent one-quarter of all mammals worldwide!

Bushy-tailed wood rats (also called pack rats) can always be found around the cave entrance—and most other cave entrances or rocky crevices in the mountains. They are extremely inquisitive and show little fear of human visitors. One is immediately struck by the ubiquitous presence of these rodents at the entrance. Large nesting piles have been built in crevices and on ledges, and these contain many items discarded or lost by hikers or cavers. Toward the fall the nests fill with vegetation and surprisingly, fungi. The Rocky Mountain maple, growing in the shelter of the canyon, is a favourite food source along with conifers, other vegetation and fungi. To obtain calcium, they chew on bones found in the cave. Sometimes our cave-touring guests are worried about rats in the cave. The name connotes swarms of them with their pointy noses and naked tails! Fortunately, we are often able to see a few of these creatures and immediately the negative rat image is disspelled, for they are a rather attractive, guinea pig-sized hamster with a long furry (not naked!) tail. Occasionally we observe young ones roaming around discovering their dark world. Active in all seasons, they live to an age of about four years.

Pack rats have large black nocturnal eyes highly suited to the dark. However, in the total darkness of the cave their eyes can no longer function and they navigate by using their long, sensitive whiskers (vibrissae) or by sniffing out trails of urine droplets. They can move very quickly in this totally dark world, climbing up overhanging walls to reach crevices. Their

A COMMON NAME LIST OF INSECTS, ARACHNIDS AND WORMS FOUND IN RAT'S NEST CAVE

INSECTS
Fungus gnats
Dark-winged fungus gnats
Gall gnats
Winter crane flies
Wingless crane flies (*Chionea obtusa*)
Heleomyzid flies
Moth flies
Small dung flies
Minute black scavenger flies
Rove beetles
Scarab beetles
Feathery wing beetles (the smallest beetles)
Cave crickets
Noctoid moths
Springtails

ARACHNIDS
Mites
Rodent fleas
Spiders (three families)
Daddy long-legs or harvesters (*Nelima paessleri*)
Rock crawlers/ice-crawlers/ice-roaches
(*Grylloblatta campodeiformis campodeiformis*)

WORMS
earthworms   By Heidi Macklin, 2000

climbing skills are legendary and I have seen their nests hundreds of metres up in crevices on vertical rock climbs. Pack rats appear to have travelled a kilometre or more into the cave, although they may have gained access by other routes, especially at the end of the Great Western Highway and Ranger Way where their remains have been found far from the entrance. The cave provides protection from predators, but the pack rats must go outside to forage and there coyotes, martens and the like can take them. Living at the entrance, they are certainly vulnerable to predators. One winter I was coming up the canyon to go into the cave when I saw a pure-white ermine dragging a limp pack rat, larger than itself, through the snow.

The Dead

Seven thousand years ago, a cougar dragged a bighorn sheep carcass into the shelter of the cave entrance to devour it. Later, smaller animals scavenged the remains, and as the carcass got dismembered, parts of it fell down the shaft. Another time a lone wolf or a bear wandered into the cave entrance. The animal was old and died there and scavengers again pushed the bones around, with some disappearing down the entrance shaft. Three thousand years ago native Indian hunters prepared the hide of a deer and packed up the meat. The unwanted bones were tossed into the pit, a convenient garbage disposal. One thousand years ago, an osprey flew up into the cave, carrying a fish from the Bow River in its talons. Picked clean, the complete fish skeleton ended up in the pit. Post-war hikers opened up their sandwiches and tossed the newspaper wrapping into the pit, Homo sapiens at the cave after an interval of 3000 years. Now, while these scenarios are somewhat fanciful, they are broadly based in fact. All and more have been

Dr. James Burns sampling the Bone Bed. Photo Dave Thomson.

Elk bones in Ranger Way. Photo Ian Drummond.

found at the bottom of the entrance pit, a veritable treasure trove of bones and other material spanning 7000 years or more.

When my partner, Tonny Hansen, and I were lobbying to get the cave declared a Provincial Historic Resource, it was necessary to inventory the cave contents to see what was worth protecting. Dr. James A. Burns, curator of Quaternary paleontology at the Provincial Museum of Alberta, was brought in to study the bones at the bottom of the entrance pit. It did not take an expert to see that the pit was important. Bones had spilled out from the base of the pit into the horizontal passage beyond. There, among ribs, vertebrae and other remains were skulls—one of a black bear, several bighorn sheep and other smaller ones. The Bone Bed itself is a 2 m-thick sequence at the base of this 15 m shaft. It is composed of layers of frost shattered rock, soil and many, many bones. One day at the bed Jim pulled out a jawbone from about halfway down the sequence: a Canadian gray wolf, by way of a preliminary assessment he suggested it was around 3000 years old.

It appears the Bone Bed may have a continuous environmental record for the last 7000 years or more. Jim has recovered a large sample of what he refers to as subfossil material, including: vertebrate bones, teeth, scales, pollen, plant macrofossils (twigs, needles, seeds and cone bracts) and insect parts. The accompanying table, which is only a preliminary list, gives you an idea of the richness of the deposit. The museum now houses vertebrate specimens. Incredibly, 34 mammalian species have been identified, including such animals as the swift fox, which is locally extinct. Many remains of birds, fish, snakes and several amphibians are also present. The

34 identified species of mammals represent a high proportion of mammals in the region (that is, 34 out of a possible 51). In addition, the identification of the now extinct passenger pigeon (among many other avian bones) fits in with historic records of this essentially eastern bird occurring in Alberta and British Columbia. This includes remains found in Eagle Cave in the Crowsnest Pass. Passenger pigeons were hunted to extinction by 1914. Two prehistoric tools have also been found dating back 3000 years (see the next chapter).

Fortunately, it is possible to date bone material by extracting the proteinaceous collagen from it. The collagen is then dated by the Carbon-14 radioisotope method. In so-doing, Dr. Dave Arnold of the Alberta Environment Radioisotopes Laboratory in Vegreville has assayed a range of samples spanning 7060 to 2480 years Before Present, but there is some mixing, especially in the top layers, which makes it difficult to define particular strata. Certainly, younger material is likely to be found; after all a 1950's fragment of newspaper was recovered in the top layers. Finding older debris is possible too, as we know the valley has been free of glacier ice for at least 13,000 years. The Bone Bed site, with its multiple lines of evidence, had the potential to provide the best-documented, mid- to late-Holocene record of environmental change anywhere in Alberta. How did animals reestablish themselves following the last intense glacial period? The spectrum of material may help to determine this. Despite the potential of the Bone Bed, regrettably much of the material has been mixed by the passage of careless cavers. A careful reexamination of the remaining sediments may reveal undisturbed pockets of material worthy of study.

In addition to the Bone Bed, bone and other organic debris is scattered through the cave. Some material has been identified, but not in detail. Many of the bones have been carried into the cave by pack rats. The bones are gnawed to rounded or facetted nodules. Otherwise, bones have accumulated from animals that entered the cave and died there, such as the coyote at the end of Coyote Descent almost 1 km into the cave. Some bat remains and numerous pack rat skeletons (e.g., at Pack Rat Grave Pit) are found deep in the cave and occasionally there are surprises, such as a crow mandible in the Wedding Cake Passage, a long way from the entrance.

Elk bones are found at the end of the Ranger Way, which may be wolf-carried, suggesting a pre-glacial entrance to the cave existed, but is now blocked. Tenacious as pack rats are, it is hard to imagine them dragging these large bones all the way from the present entrance. If another entrance existed, it is now more than likely mantled by the extensive glacial terraces that lap the flanks of the Bow Valley. However, fresh pack rat skeletons and the presence of bats at the end of the Great West Highway, above those terraces, may mean an entrance currently open.

A PRELIMINARY LIST OF SPECIES FROM RAT'S NEST CAVE

INSECTIVORA (shrews, etc.)
Sorex cf. S. arcticus (Arctic shrew)
Sorex sp. (shrew)

CHIROPTERA (bats)
Lasionycteris noctivagans (silver-haired bat)
Unidentified bat (little brown?)

LAGOMORPHA (pikas, hares, etc.)
Ochotona princeps (pika)
Lepus americanus (hare)

RODENTIA (rodents)
Marmota caligata (hoary marmot)
Spermophilius columbianus (Columbian ground squirrel)
Eutamius sp. (chipmunk)
Tamiasciurus hudsonicus (red squirrel)
Peromyscus maniculatus (deer mouse)
Neotoma cinerea (bushy-tailed wood rat)
Clethrionomys gapperi (red-backed vole)
Phenacomys intermedius (heather vole)
Microtus sp. (vole)
Erethizon dorsatum (porcupine)

CARNIVORA (carnivores)
Ursus americanus (black bear)
Canis lupus (gray wolf)
Canis latrans (coyote)
Vulpes velox (swift fox)
Mustela vison (mink)
Martes americana (pine marten)
Gulo gulo (wolverine)
Taxidea taxus (badger)
Mustelidae sp. (weasel)
Lynx canadensis (lynx)
Unidentified

ARTIODACTYLA (even-toed ruminants)
Odocoileus sp. (deer)
Cervus elaphus (wapiti or elk)
Bison bison (plains bison)
Ovis canadensis (bighorn sheep)

AVES (birds)—includes passenger pigeon, crow and golden eagle
PISCES (fish)
AMPHIBIA (frogs and salamanders)
REPTILIA (snakes)

By Dr. James Burns, 1986

9 Human Presence: Pelican Lake Culture

"There is almost nowhere in this province that does not bear the residue of Alberta's ancient peoples," Michael Payne, Director of Historical Resources, Alberta Culture

We know from archaeological diggings at the Vermilion Lake site, Banff, that people have inhabited the region continuously from historic times to 10,500 years Before Present (or BP). Thirteen of such sites have been investigated. But it seems that much earlier, possibly even as early as the mid-Wisconsin 60,000-25,000 years ago, the Americas may have been peopled from Asia. These hunter-gatherers could have crossed the Bering Strait during glacial sea level lowering, and followed the so-called Ice-free Corridor southward, eventually spreading throughout the North and South American continents. The Ice-free Corridor seems to have persisted throughout most of the Pleistocene glaciations and existed where two great ice masses—one from the Canadian Shield and one from the Western Cordillera—just failed to collide.

While the bone deposits at Rat's Nest Cave date back more than 7000 years BP and mineral deposits much earlier, evidence of humans at the site is relatively recent. Thus far, only two human artifacts, a point (dart tip) and a projectile point-base, have been recovered. The point has characteristic notching and has been assigned to the Pelican Lake style (circa 1350 BC–100 AD) by Jack Brink and Bob Dawe of the Archaeological Survey of Alberta. Apparently, new peoples had infiltrated the region at this time. Their tools were more advanced than hitherto used. Notching of points, for example, meant that they could be more firmly attached to wooden shafts.

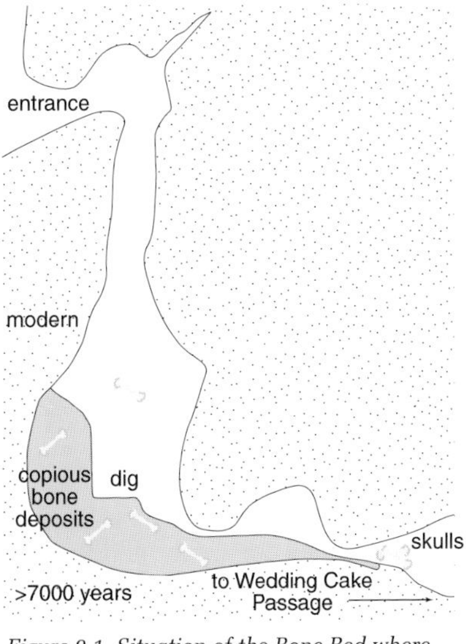

More than 5000 years ago in the Alberta region people practised a communal style of hunting where buffalo herds were driven over cliffs or bluffs. The buffalo thus killed would be butchered for food and other materials for living. Around 4200-3500 years BP (a period assigned to the so-called McKean Complex), there seems to have been an abandonment of the buffalo jump method of hunting. Based on evidence from the celebrated

Figure 9.1. Situation of the Bone Bed where many mammal remains were found.

Circa 3000 year-old Pelican Lake Point from the Bone Bed. Photo Archaeological Survey of Alberta.

Head-Smashed-In Buffalo Jump and other sites, the McKean peoples only sporadically utilized them. At around 3300 years BP, mass kills at Head-Smashed-In and other buffalo jump sites resumed. The new peoples had arrived, and mainly because they resurrected the art of buffalo jumps they are referred to as "the Renaissance People of the Plains." (These same people are the ones that appear to have visited Rat's Nest Cave.) At this time the Alberta Plains likely looked much the same as when Europeans arrived. The northern forests had pushed southward to their present position and the grasslands, which had extended northward to the Saskatchewan River, had evolved into mixed parkland forest. The new groups of people spread onto the Plains, reusing the buffalo jumps, and fashioned tools identified as the Pelican Lake style (from a site in south central Saskatchewan).

The projectile point or dart tip found at Rat's Nest Cave is fashioned from a rock known as the "Banff chert," a misnomer for the fact that it is a silicified, banded siltstone with alternating black and brownish bands. This material is readily available locally. In fact, one archaeological site in the Spray Lakes area, south of Canmore, yielded thousands of flakes and tools of this rock-type, suggestive of a convenient local source. The characteristic notching of the point suggests a strong parallel with the Pelican Lake point type. While this type is usually found in sites situated on the Plains, one site near Sundre, Alberta, has yielded many that are indistinguishable from those called "Pelican Lake" elsewhere. One suggestion is that the Rat's Nest Cave specimen, and those from around Sundre, may represent a montane variant of the common Plains point.

In any event, among the tools found from this period on the Plains are: sharply triangular, deeply corner-notched projectiles, end scrapers, ovoid bifaces, chipped stone drills and bone artifacts. Because the type of projectile (lance or dart tip) is a fairly common find in Alberta, it has been suggested the population density had begun to increase significantly at this time. In any event, the sophistication associated with these tools suggests a broader culture than had hitherto existed, and where contact and trade with other groups may have been far reaching. For example, some tools were made from obsidian, a volcanic basaltic glass whose closest provenance is Wyoming or Oregon. This may be the case for the projectile point-base found at Rat's Nest. It was identified as having been made from green obsidian by Don Prosser, then a government geologist and Alberta Speleological Society member. Its origin (provenance) is not known, but it most likely came from Oregon or Washington, and is unlikely to have come from B.C.

In addition to making sophisticated tools, the Pelican Lake peoples created beautifully fashioned ornaments of shells and buried their dead in shallow cairn-covered graves. Much more so than their predecessors, the Pelican Lake users left distinctive signs of their temporary camps in the form of tipi rings. These stone circles probably held down the flaps of their cone-shaped tents. Literally thousands of tipi rings have been found, and can still be discovered, on the southern Alberta Plains. No such sites have been found in the vicinity of Rat's Nest Cave, but it is likely that the cave would have afforded shelter for hunting trips into the mountains. The tipis would have been heavy and awkward to transport through the mountainous terrain.

Despite the relative sophistication of these people, it seems they didn't possess pottery and whether they used the bow and arrow is controversial. Perhaps they made do with the dart and spear thrower (atlatl). Nonetheless, it has been suggested smaller Pelican Lake style points may have been used as arrowheads. Conventional wisdom has it that the bow and arrow did not become widely used as a weapon in the region until around 1800 years ago. Therefore, Pelican Lake points appear to be anachronisms. It could be that the bow and arrow were used much earlier than previously thought.

As the end of the so-called middle Prehistoric period approached, the Pelican Lake style of point seems to have disappeared from the Plains. It had lasted a thousand years. It's possible they may have adopted new technologies, or perhaps they just moved away. In any event, the successive Plains dwellers used two new styles known as Besant and Avonlea. Both are known for their highly refined bison hunting cultures.

One more piece of evidence might suggest later aboriginal presence at the cave. Above the entrance shaft (down which the artifacts were found) there is just the ghost of an ochre smear. Could there have been pictographs here, which were effaced by the rising vapour from the cave? Grotto Canyon, an impressive feature with steep corridor-like walls, defines the east margin of Grotto Mountain. On one wall of the canyon there are pictographs drawn in red ochre. Above Canmore, at Grassi Lakes there are likewise pictographs. Scenes often depict successful battles or hunts. Evidence from a site called Writing-on-Stone suggests that at a maximum, pictographs are not more than 1000 years old. The question remains whether the ochre writing technology came about prior to 1000 years or whether the ochre simply will not survive longer than this period. In any event, it seems unlikely that aboriginal activity at the cave ceased with the Pelican Lake peoples 3000 years ago.

Our story from Rat's Nest Cave, however, breaks for a considerable time here, at least as far as we know, and resumes in the following chapter with the Europeans in 1858 AD—the famed Palliser Expedition.

10 The Mystery of Hector's Cave

Our history now moves from aboriginal use of the cave some thousand years ago and more, to the early European explorers. While the Bow Valley corridor in the vicinity of Banff saw the odd early European traveller, the first fully documented accounts are those of the Palliser Expedition (1857-1860). And their exploits have left us with the enigma of a disappearing cave!

Sponsored by the Royal Geographical Society of London, John Palliser, an Irishman, received a grant of 5000 pounds to mount an expedition to western North America. The objective was to find and survey suitable routes across the southern portion of the Rocky Mountains. The RGS requested he take a number of scientists and technical men with him to undertake a range of scientific activities, which apart from the survey included biological and geological inventories, meteorology and geomagnetic measurements. The latter activity was part of an international study of the earth's magnetic field.

Of relevance to this account, we pick up Palliser's travels after the expedition had been split into two groups so that a wider range of exploration could be entertained. Understandable, as they had a 500 km-long mountain barrier to explore! While Palliser was gearing up to travel southward to the Kananaskis area, expedition members Dr. James Hector and Eugene Bourgeau pushed on up the Bow River. Hector was a 23 year-old medical

View of Graymont's quarry seen from Canmore.

doctor from Edinburgh University used to making rugged trips into his native mountains. He was also a keen amateur naturalist and geologist. Bourgeau was a botanist from the French Alps and likewise was inured to rugged mountain travel. He was reputedly a very amiable individual, liked by all—a happy choice for the expedition.

Once beyond the Kananaskis River tributary, Hector's and Bourgeau's trail up the Bow Valley passed through fine, open woods of young pine and over high, level terraces. Then the valley narrowed (where the Bow cuts through the Front Ranges) giving their horses a lot of trouble with mounds of rounded cobbles swept in by torrents from steep side valleys. Also the surrounding forests were dense, making progress very difficult in the deadfall. Eventually they could look down over Lac des Arcs to Grotto Mountain (both names given by Bourgeau), and through the Bow Valley gap in the Fairholme Range to comparatively open valley-floor montane ahead—the current site of Canmore. Grotto Mountain may have been so-named because of the many cave entrances seen from the valley bottom, or because of the cave they apparently discovered there. It seems they may have camped at Gap Lake, in which case they were directly below the southeast end of Grotto Mountain.

On August 12, 1858, Hector and Bourgeau went exploring above the timberline on Grotto Mountain directly behind their camp. Hector wrote:

"At dawn started with Bourgeau to ascend Grotto Mountain. Passed over rugged ledges of blue limestone, which weathers to a light blue colour, and is traversed by veins of calc spar. The surface of these beds is very rough, and masses of chert are left protruding by the action of the weather. After ascending 500 feet we get out of the timber…."

At this point Bourgeau began to collect alpine plants, noteworthy of which was saxifrage (he later found 10 kinds in the Rocky Mountains). They continued upward, by following a "torrent" to where progress was barred by a trickle of water falling several hundred feet, at the base of which they washed-up in a mossy-banked pool. Hector reported:

"On one side of this little valley there is a deposit of angular blocks of rock, mixed with calcareous clay, forming the sides to a height of 150 feet. In this deposit we found a large cave, with a high arched roof and narrow mouth, and like Robinson Crusoe's one, with an old goat for a tenant, but in this case he had been long dead. The floor was quite battered hard by the tracks of sheep and goats.

"Turning from this point, which was 1000 feet above camp, we descended by another spur of the mountain for breakfast."

Now while the trickle falling several hundred feet could well fit the small valley containing Rat's Nest Cave—it does indeed have such a feature albeit probably less than 100 feet—the cave itself does not fit their description. Rat's Nest Cave is solidly encased in massive limestone and has a low wide arch. Inside a smooth sloping floor of rock is punched through by a 15 m pit. Furthermore, a careful reading of their account suggests they had not yet travelled along the southwest flank of the mountain, which they would have to have done to reach the Rat's Nest Valley.

Later in the day, having separated from Bourgeau who went off collecting on Wind Mountain across the Bow, Hector reported:

"Our track led over the spur of Grotto Mountain, from the limestone of which I collected some fossil shells [Productus, etc.]. We then entered the great valley, which runs NW and is several miles in width. We kept for several miles high up on the side of it, skirting along high banks of the terraced deposits which had been preserved from erosion by the spur we had just crossed."

This suggests they crossed the Rat's Nest Valley as they travelled northwest along the main Bow Valley on the south-facing flank of Grotto Mountain to eventually camp close to the present site of Canmore at Indian Flats. Furthermore, he describes hoodoos, of which there is a very fine example in a quarry below Rat's Nest Cave (hoodoos are pillars of remnant glacial-alluvial sediments capped by a hard layer that protects them from erosion).

One other possibility for the elusive cave is one up Grotto Canyon, but several details do not fit. The canyon is not above timberline and one does not have to ascend bands of limestone to get to it. It does, however, contain a trickle at a prominent split in the canyon's watercourse (a favourite for ice climbers when it forms up in the winter) and a cave in glacial till farther up valley, which might fit Hector's description. One wonders if two accounts have somehow been merged into one. After all, Grotto Canyon is a very prominent feature defining the eastern margin of Grotto Mountain and it would seem almost surprising if they had not ventured into it.

Where else could they have gone? Two other possibilities are on the southeast face of Grotto Mountain right above their camp—trickles there maybe, but no cave has been reported, and then there's Stephen Canyon. Stephen Canyon is the next drainage east of Grotto Canyon. It cuts back up into the long ridge of Mount Fable in a series of waterfalls, and it offers rocky spurs on each side for ascent and descent. However, no caves have been reported from this site either. Grotto Mountain has numerous cave entrances that can be seen from the Trans-Canada Highway. Some have been investigated, but so far all of them but Rat's Nest are little more than alcoves. One day we may find Hector's lost cave, or perhaps decide that we already know where it is. In any event, seeing the extent of Rat's Nest Cave, other long cave systems may yet be found under the mountain.

11 Modern Exploration
Pull out the cave map and follow the explorers

"Are you through yet?" said Dave, impatiently lying flat out in the body-sized tube that we had been excavating over several weekends.

"Yes, I can see into a large black space, but I need to widen it a bit," replied Norman, who lay two body-lengths ahead. "So you'll just have wait."

Meanwhile, I was languishing in hospital waiting for a cartilage operation on my knee after a caving fall in Central America. It was 1987. Knowing that we were close to breaking through to new passageways, I was dying to know what they had found. About six months earlier, I had been on a trip up the Wedding Cake Passage (so-called because of a stalagmite of that shape growing there). We had got to the end and were just about to turn round when Jon Rollins detected a miniscule draft coming from a place where mud had almost filled the passage to the ceiling. The draft promised more cave beyond what was a sediment blocked U-tube. Over the next few weekends we dug away labouriously at the mud floor for hours at a time. Our first success was to break through into a tiny chamber, a small respite that

made it easier to dig onward. I had "borrowed" a University of Calgary Food Services tray to which were attached two lengths of rope, one at each end. Digging proceeded by cleaving out dollops of stratified mud and plonking them on the tray. This was hauled back and dumped, and then hauled back in again for the next load. The person at the front, meanwhile, was lying flat out and had to do some peculiar contortions to send the filled tray back under his/her body. It was fairly boring for the person doing the dumping, but fortunately the mud had a beautiful consistency for molding. The result was a number of figurines of a diabolical nature carefully crafted from the clay—the devil's bust has survived to this day!

Curtain stalactites and stalagmites close to the Bone Bed.

Well, Norman Flux and Dave Thomson did get through what they subsequently dubbed the "Birth Canal" and entered into a good-sized passage trending upward into the unknown. No one had ever been there before and this is always a tremendously exciting moment in caving. On return trips over the next few months, a number of members from the Alberta Speleological Society explored more than 1.5 km of passageways there.

Early Trips

The earliest record of modern activity at Rat's Nest Cave is in the 1950s. We know this from a fragment of newspaper found at the bottom of the entrance pit. Of course, we recognize that humans have been at the cave entrance for more than 3000 years (see Chapter 9). Serious exploration began in the early 1970s following rumours from mountain climbers in the Banff and Canmore area of a cave on Grotto Mountain. In fact, the climbers referred to it somewhat tautologically as "Grotto Cave," an alternative name still used.

The Alberta Speleological Society, active since the early 1960s, and always interested in any reports of new caves, checked out the rumour. With directions from local climbers, Gary Pilkington and Ian Drummond of the ASS found the prominent entrance. They immediately descended the Bone Bed shaft only to find the bottom plugged with rocks, dirt and old bones. The cave was written off at that point.

Local climbers led by a climber also in the ASS returned to the cave and found a lead at the top of the shaft almost completely blocked by pack rat nests (this inspired them to

Negotiating a passage near the Bone Bed pit. Photo Ian Drummond.

Column formation beyond the Birth Canal. Photo Ian Drummond.

name the cave Rat's Nest Cave). The story goes that they saw a pack rat disappear and pulling out the nesting material exposed a short crawlway leading to a down-climb. Entering, they soon found themselves at the top of the large wedge-shaped first chamber, which is about 17 m long—they had clearly got into something significant.

Bugs McKeith with ASS members Diana Knaak and Mike Boon (a legendary character of international caving fame) scrambled down to the far end of the chamber. They then climbed up into a round opening, and followed a left-leaning fissure passage to the brink of a pit (the one rappelled down on our tours). Looking across the pit, they were impressed by the far wall coated in a brilliant-white deposit of moonmilk.

The ASS made short work of exploring the passages on this side of the system (actually most of our tour route). Warmer than most other Rockies' caves, and lacking the usual deep, multiple descents, loose piles of frost-shattered rock so common elsewhere, it seemed a rather friendly place. They found that the moonmilk pit emptied into a large descending passage. Observing the pockets and pendants in the roof, excitement mounted when they realized they were in a substantial conduit that had once been full of flowing water, but flowing from where? Farther on they entered the Grand Gallery, the largest chamber in the cave system, where they first saw soda straws and other formations high up on the ceiling. Descending through the floor of the chamber, they passed by mineral encrusted walls leading to a beautifully decorated grotto ending at a siphon. The explorers could go no farther and it would be much later before scuba divers pushed past the siphon, as described ahead. (It was to be much later before each end of the fault that cuts through the Grand Gallery was pushed. A crawlway at the south end was pushed through two squeezes to an extremely tight fissure. This last obstacle was passed by Pam Yonge and Marg Saul of the ASS and

A low space near the end of the Wedding Cake Passage.

later widened and pushed to an end at 40 m. At the north end of the Grand Gallery, Dave Thompson and I bolted our way up to the ceiling where it rises over 30 m. Although a good air movement is encountered here, we have thus far found no way to go forward.)

Returning from the Grand Gallery the early team followed a smaller left fork they'd noticed earlier. Forced onto hands and knees, they followed the series of squeezes and climbs including the Treacherous Slab until they ended more than 40 m down a large, steeply dipping tube blocked by sandy sediments (currently being dug). Backing up, however, they found a small drafting tube leading off at head height. This, the Hose-pipe Passage, would mark a new level of endeavour. Regrettably, neither Gary nor Bugs lived to experience further exploration. Gary died with Ekhart Grassman during a spectacular fall while attempting a difficult route on Mount Edith Cavell, and Bugs was killed falling through a cornice on the summit of Mount Assiniboine during a whiteout.

Suddenly the cave had got harder and more serious and other members of the ASS got involved. Descending a series of steeply dipping, body-sized tubes and pushing through a number of squeezes brought them to a point where the roof descended to the surface of a pool (the end of our High Adventure Tour). Kim Smallwood, Eric Neilson and Wes Davies of the ASS then siphoned the pool using a garden hose (hence the name Hose-pipe Passage). This allowed onward progress, if rather wet. The first person through was John Donovan, an inveterate caver hailing from England who returned with Eric and two other ASS members. Sliding on their backs through the pool, nose pressed against the ceiling, they gained an even more tortuous series of tubes and squeezes. At this point John continued alone ascending to a large passage (the Wedding Cake Passage). Going rightward quickly brought him to a rubble-blocked end. Scattered around were

Caver exploring new section beyond the Birth Canal. Photo Ian Drummond.

skulls of bighorn sheep, a bear skull and many bones—he had reached the base of the entrance pit!

Later trips involving the same individuals but further supported by Peter Thompson, Linda Hastie and Don Prosser followed the route taken by John. However, this time taking the leftward route that went through a series of upward and downward trending tubes of a good size, before passing through a beautifully decorated section. The floor gleamed with crystal that had clearly formed underwater (The Frozen River) and thick multi-coloured mineral columns had the appearance of supporting the roof. Forests of soda straws hung from the ceiling. Eventually the passage ended at a prominent stalagmite, which they christened the Wedding Cake. A downward lead toward the end, the only possibility left at this point, was not pushed hard. The trip back to the entrance was long and arduous, seriously depleting enthusiasm for exploration. The cave, then about 1.5 km in length, was mapped during several trips in 1979, but its location and the map were kept under wraps. Compared to other caves in the Rockies, Rat's Nest Cave is so very accessible that there was (and is!) understandable concern for its preservation.

After finding such a well-decorated passage in the Wedding Cake, there was controversy in the ASS because the entrance pit had been dug into (from the inside). The fear was that easy access would lead to formations being damaged—a fear all too well founded, as it turned out. The ease of access resulted in a further wave of exploration, but not until later. Inevitably, too, the secret of the cave's location gradually got out, and people visited the cave in increasing numbers. Some guiding was also being done in the early 1980s. Regrettably, some damage has occurred to the formations since then, some of which have been removed, and all of the skulls have disappeared from the Bone Bed pit. Unlike Cadomin Cave to the north, Rat's Nest has fortunately suffered only minimally from graffiti.

Scuba Diving

In the spring of 1979, with the cave seemingly fully explored, interest turned to the siphon at the Grotto. A cave diver, Paul Hadfield of British origin, entered the 5°C water in full scuba gear and managed to get through to an airspace on the other side. Although he had dived to a depth of only 3 m and had reached the other side within 15 m, it had proved to be a technical dive in a constricted passage—such dives should never be underestimated. At one time cave diving was one of the most dangerous activities around and the fatality rate has been compared to Himalayan climbing. In my 30 years of caving I have personally known four people lost to cave dives—one a very close friend, Derek Tringham, who did not return from a cave dive in Spain and his body was never found. Now that there are courses for cave divers and cave divers are better trained, there are fewer fatalities, which emphasizes that open-water divers should never attempt this. The obvious danger is that a diver cannot surface if something goes wrong. Although one lays a line to be followed on the return, fine sediment stirred up invariably reduces visibility to centimetres—lines can be lost, or cut if the diver gets tangled, and without guidance the diver may swim into oblivion as the air

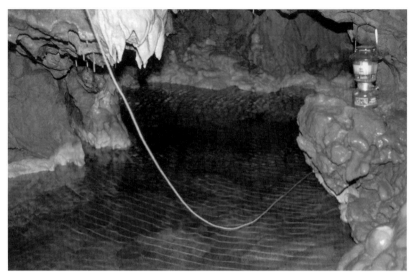

The first siphon leading from the Grotto. Note dive line. Photo Dave Thomson.

runs out. This last is the most common cause of death, and was the cause of my good friend's death. Added to all of this is that siphons (or sumps) are very often constricted necessitating the diver to side-mount the bottles. Valves can be damaged or turned off if they drag against the ceiling.

With all of these considerations in mind, and because he did not have a buddy, Paul stopped at a second siphon. He returned in 1980 with Tom Barton, who had a miserable time in the first sump:

"I had borrowed an ill-fitting wetsuit and was very cold. The result was a heavy consumption of air in my bottle. My light decided to go along with the poor conditions and quit...."

They did not continue, but returned in the summer to have more success. Backed by a good Sherpa team, which is invariably needed for carting the heavy equipment through the cave, they also filmed the dive. On reaching the second siphon, they found it to be longer (18 m) and even more constricted than the first, upping the seriousness. Once through, however, they found the cave opened up into a large rounded passage trending downward at 10° and ending at a 10 m down-climb into a pool—almost a siphon—with a nose-sized airspace over the top. Having negotiated the pool they were confronted by a complete change in the cave's character—the rounded passage continued on as a high fissure, narrow at its base and difficult to move along. That was enough and they turned back. But fired by the excitement of discovery, Tom was back within two weeks with a Sherpa team and film crew. He climbed into the top of the rift for easier passage, although caution was needed because of some loose boulders, but was then stopped at its end by a cascade falling into space, obscuring his view to the bottom.

A week later he was back with Randy Spahl from the ASS and a couple of 10 m flexible ladders. Randy had buoyancy problems so he stopped at the second sump while Tom continued. The ladders hung shy of the bottom of the cascade by about 2 m, which he free-climbed, only to be confronted by a fourth siphon. Having left his diving gear back at the start of the rift (it was hard enough getting through the rift without any equipment), Tom swam about in the pool, but could find no way on over the top. A week later they returned but exhaustion forced them back before they could investigate it—this was not easy exploration! Finally, at the end of the summer, Tom once again pushed through the siphons with another ASS member, Dayle Gilliat. Now they found the ladder to be hung up and jammed between boulders; another aborted trip!

It wasn't until 1988 or '89 when Tom, together with experienced cave diver David Sawatsky, returned well equipped to tackle the fourth sump. I was one of the "Sherpas" who had the misfortune to drag in the heavy gear for that trip. Having successfully negotiated all the difficulties, they got to the final sump and quickly found two openings leading off somewhere. Both leads, however, were too tight to follow, which has finished the exploration there. In all, these intrepid individuals explored 200 m of passage getting to a depth of 80 m, one of the deepest points in the cave.

The scuba-diving story does not end here, as there are other places to dive in the cave. In 1997 Istvan Szlany of the ASS dived a remote siphon in the Rabbit Warren. This trip was particularly hard for the Sherpas, and resulted in only 7 m of underwater passage. The way on is too tight at a constriction fringed by jagged rocks. Just one other prospect for diving remains at the bottom of the Ranger Way where a large pool appears to harbour a passage leading off under the far wall. We can expect a yet harder carry for the Sherpas when this is attempted.

Tom Barton returns successfully from having dived the siphons at the Grotto.
Photo Dave Thomson.

Wedding Cake Passage and Caverns Measureless...

Toward the end of the 1980s, when I was doing an inventory study for the Alberta Historic Resources Foundation after the cave had been declared a Provincial Historic Resource, we made a major breakthrough in the cave. This was in digging out the Birth Canal described at the beginning of this chapter. With the Wedding Cake Passage heading into the core of Grotto Mountain, we were clearly moving toward the ancient source of water that had created these passages. The nearest point of this source could, at a minimum, be on the other side of the mountain in Cougar Creek 5 km distant, if not farther. Once Dave and Norman had broken through the psychologically taxing Birth Canal and had quickly assessed the passages beyond, several of us followed on a number of explorative forays over the next few weeks. Our names, among other names, appear on the cave map. Ian McKenzie, Jon Rollins, Randy Spahl, Bill MacDonald and I were the main proponents during this phase of exploration. We mapped and photographed the passages as we went. Photography meant that we recorded the scenery prior to our impacting it, as these passageways had yet to see a human being.

In the pristine passages they had initially pushed, Norman and Dave had found the formations to be unblemished by mud and careless breakage. Clusters of soda-straws and hair-like helictites reflected back the lights, gleaming brilliantly white. From the Birth Canal, crawling passage trends upward to break into a chamber, which contains these formations. They had proceeded onward stooping-fashion to reach the Terminus, a large rectangular-shaped chamber containing Stonehenge-like blocks that had fallen from the roof. These had fallen a long time ago when the cave had drained out, relieving these roof blocks of their bouyancy. Although there were many nooks and crannies to be investigated, and a steady draft to entice them onward, they could not find a way out of the room other than the way they had come in. That was until they climbed back over the top into a crawling passage that ended as roof nearly met floor. The floor was covered in mud, dry and cracked, which meant they could cleave slabs from the floor.

Quickly they got through to the base of a long, large-diameter tube leading quite steeply upward (the Slimy Climb). The mud-caked slope was very slippery, but they managed to ascend it—this time. Subsequently, with the passage of boots it became more treacherous and a hand-line has been fitted. Once up the climb, they encountered a passage increasing in height, canyon-like, making it some of the largest in the cave. Beyond, the passage continued as a sloping slot, ascending and descending through stunning areas of formations, some honey-coloured, some gleaming white. They reached a chamber containing hefty, squat stalagmites and a nest of cave pearls with a couple of passages onward. They took the obvious one, which was large, and with surprise passed a dead pack rat that still possessed its skin. How long had that been there? Are we approaching another entrance, they thought? Finally the intrepid duo entered a large room (the High Point) with shaft holes in the ceiling and a yawning chasm in the floor.

Digging out the Birth Canal. Photo Dave Thomson.

The cave should have kept going upward toward the source, why was it diving downward? Without ropes they were unable to continue and called it a day. The survey eventually revealed that they had gained 80 m in elevation from the entrance.

The next phase of exploration saw several long trips up to 10 hours in length, with ropes and survey equipment. As my knee was sufficiently recovered, I was able to rejoin the initiative, which involved a fair cross-section of the ASS (Dave Thomson, Jon Rollins and Bill MacDonald). It was a fairly easy traverse around the chasm at the High Point chamber and a small streamway led off on the other side, but soon choked with silt and flowstone. We checked one of the holes in the roof but it pinched out too. Recently (in 2000), Jason Morgan and Heidi Macklin checked the largest hole in the ceiling of the High Point, lying right over the chasm. After exciting and exposed climbing they unfortunately discovered that it pinched out. The way on is definitely downward.

The chasm itself was descended for 40 m, the longest drop yet found in the cave, but it ended, choked with mud. Deep mud pits, lined with calcite, were very notable, formed by drips having fallen from the lofty ceiling. After an initial disappointment, we found a way on about halfway down the pit. A small swing on the rope and we were into a passageway. Almost immediately a climb presented itself on the left, but leaving this to a later date, we continued down the passage. The passage then swung through 180°. More mud pits were found on the bend. This took us into the Pearly Way where another lead was temporarily ignored on the left (the Rabbit Warren).

Why the Pearly Way? Exquisite nests of cave pearls were found here, the first sighting in the cave. In some nests the pearls were tiny and multitudinous, but in others large. As the passage continued, we were very careful not to disturb them. Interestingly, we found claw marks toward the end of this passage, and then heard the tinkling of a stream. The stream descended from an impenetrable slot falling into a pool, which blocked the way. It was duly noted that the passage continued under water, and as mentioned above in the diving history, it was finally dived to a short end several years later by Istvan Szlany.

Attention then turned to the Rabbit Warren, a name inspired by its complexity. It was found, one way, to lead back by a very tortuous and damp route, over a "crystal pool" (hard to avoid getting wet) back into the main passage, thus avoiding the chasm pit. Another way led to a low, wide calcified chamber off which led the Sucker Route, an arduous, low, painful crawlway that required a lot of enthusiasm. Randy (of diving fame) and I named it with some asperity after being told it was a good lead (even though it seemed to be heading back into the main passage). After considerable effort, we finally got to where the others had stopped, and were able to grovel forward for another 10 m. The crawl became inconclusively small at a little pile of droppings, which seemed an appropriate place to beat a retreat!

The next few trips concentrated on the climb close to the halfway point on the 40 m pit. We found this to lead to a series of crystalline pools. We were shortly stopped by one of these; well, we weren't prepared to take a bath as the ceiling fell to within a few centimetres of the water. This meant a return trip with a length of hose and we successfully lowered the water enough to stay reasonably dry. Soon after, we were confronted by a narrow

Negotiating the Birth Canal. Photo Dave Thomson.

Surveying new passages beyond the Birth Canal. Photo Dave Thomson.

The Terminus room. Photo Dave Thomson.

slimy rift with uncompromisingly parallel walls descending for a long way (the Bastard Climb). It was not precisely a pitch, but we attached a thin line to it as obviously it was going to be very awkward to get back up. It descended for a long way, for 50 m actually, in a series of large steps and it was the scene of a great deal of cursing on the return. Finally, we had to rig a further 15 m pitch into the Mud Room, a chamber liberally coated in a thick layer of fine sediment. From here a wide walking passage descended down the fault.

We were excited because, despite the complexity of the cave at this end of the system, passages are not diminished in size here—the cave does not seem to be dispersing into smaller and smaller passageways that might reasonably end. We passed a lonely bat skeleton, prostrate on a mud bank. Again the cave changed character and we entered a long rift chamber at right angles to the large passage we had descended, and another rope pitch. This we descended for 10 m to enter a smaller passage that meandered down to a mud choke—the Ignominious End. Our survey indicates we had lost 136 m of elevation to reach this point from the top of the chasm (the High Point). But as the cave is still heading into Grotto Mountain, the water must have come from this direction, having forced upward to this height—an impressive pressure head and an indication of much passage beyond.

So where does the cave go from here? We have quite strong drafts at this end of the system, indicative of further passageways, but the frustrating fact remains that we can't seem to identify where they are coming from. It's not as if we haven't looked. For example, an excessively narrow slightly

Looking down the Slimy Climb. Photo Dave Thomson.

A dug section off the Grand Gallery. Photo David Brandreth.

Fault-oriented passage in Ranger Way. Photo Dave Thomson.

Caver among formations beyond the Birth Canal during exploration. Photo Dave Thomson.

The author descends a 40 m pitch from the High Point. Photo Dave Thomson.

drafting shaft in the Mud Room floor was descended by Sean Doherty. I can remember encouraging him when, some metres down it, muffled words of panic reached me at the top. He'd got half way round to a slight twist in the body-sized well, could not continue and was seriously worried as to whether he could get back—a long way from home to be stuck! Although we have pushed all sorts of nooks and crannies, somewhere I feel we have missed something. There is every hope and it is not an exaggeration to say that a breakthrough here could lead to kilometres of passage through Grotto Mountain. The cave still has a long way to go.

Going Deep in Rat's Nest Cave

If you're not a cave diver, you can still get to the deepest reaches of the cave. Curiously, prior to the Birth Canal breakthrough, an obvious lead just before it had not been pushed very hard. That lead eventually produced around 1 km of passage in Coyote Descent and Ranger Way.

In order to complete the survey, we wanted to map this lead in. We didn't think much was there, but it was a job and had to be done. First, we mapped a loop and noted a passage going off it (Ranger Way). Because soda straws blocked the start of the passage, a crawlway, we were a bit reluctant to break through into it. We therefore concentrated on the rather wider passage following the steep dip of the fault downward. Although wide, the passage is extremely low and to continue involves a very awkward squeeze around jammed boulders, but once through it gets higher. There are impressive curtain formations here formed by seeping water that travelled down the steeply inclined ceiling leaving a mineral trace as it went. One of them is more than 2 m long.

We were surprised to see animal remains so far into the cave. First, a bat skeleton, then pack rat bones. As we climbed steeply down we came across some large scats. What had made these? At the bottom our mystery was solved with the full skeleton of a coyote lying on a mud floor. Either this animal had come from some other entrance, or it had fallen down the entrance pit into the Bone Bed. Not dead at this point, it must have blundered around in the dark, taking it deeper and deeper into the system before it succumbed at the end of Coyote Descent—a lonely and frightening end.

Meanwhile, as we surveyed away, some rangers led by Frank Gee from Bow Valley Provincial Park had broken through the soda-straw barrier and entered Ranger Way, as it was later called. I certainly do not want to criticize them for the breakage. The fact is that we would have eventually done the same thing. They did get through with minimal damage. In fact, so much so that we found it hard not to create further damage when we went to survey their findings. The quality of formations, helictites, curtains, soda straws and large stalactites and stalagmites found perhaps justifies the exploration (see the cover of this book). I suppose it's rather an anthropocentric view that formations are valuable only if viewed by humans. There are no doubt vast quantities of undiscovered caves with similar formations in the Rockies, which by the fact they may never be entered have their formations preserved for posterity.

Descending into the Mud Room in a remote part of the cave. Photo Dave Thomson.

Ranger Way is also a very sporting passage descending in a series of climbs and chutes, actually, one of my favourites in the cave. Frank Gee and company had stopped at a boulder blockage after around 200 m, an obvious end. We were spurred on by the sight of a bat roosting and a nest containing large bones, perhaps of an elk or some animal of a similar size. Remembering the coyote, the question once again rose in our minds as to how these had got here and whether another entrance existed at one time. On repeated trips, we dug at the choke and broke through into a number of passages leading off in different directions. Continuing on down one of these, we arrived at the Low Point, a large, deep pool leading off into a siphon. Aside from the other siphons off the Grotto, we had reached the deepest point in the cave 165 m below the entrance. We may get deeper by diving the sump, but I don't envy the Sherpas that will have to cart all that heavy equipment through the cave!

Between the High Point and the Low Point, the cave has a 245 m vertical range in a length of just over 4 km making it the eleventh longest and fourteenth deepest cave in Canada. We can expect this status to change as we continue our exploration into what I believe to be a major cave system in Canada.

Ranger Way. Photo Dave Thomson.

12 Ecotourism and Management of the Cave

Few caves in the Canadian Rocky Mountains, and certainly no accessible caves, come close to matching the variety of features that make Rat's Nest Cave so popular. The cave can also be reached year-round, whereas as other caves in the Rockies have brief time windows for entry. In extreme cases, there are caves that will not even open up in high snow years. At 4 km in length, Rat's Nest Cave is the eleventh longest cave in Canada and the second longest in Alberta.

After only a five-minute drive from Canmore, a short, picturesque hike of less than 30 minutes from Highway 1A gets you to the entrance. Comparable caves in Alberta are Cadomin and Wapiabi, which involve 3-4 hours of driving from major centres and require steep avalanche-prone hikes of 1-2 hours to reach them. Of the two, only Cadomin can be reached in winter, but it is off limits because of the resident hibernating bat population. A smaller cave at Bragg Creek (Canyon Creek Ice Cave) with almost as easy access as Rat's Nest is often blocked by ice close to the entrance and has nowhere near the array of features exhibited by Rat's Nest. Nonetheless, all of these sites are experiencing an increasing number of visitors. We

A curious mud swirl formation—now extinct. Photo Dave Thomson.

currently guide around 800 persons a year at Rat's Nest, with a similar number entering the cave without authorization. This makes a total of around 1600 visitors per year and that number is increasing.

Much of the cave's appeal lies in its apparent wilderness setting. The view across the Bow Valley to the shimmering heights of Mount Lougheed and the blade-like spine of the Wind Tower is very impressive. The view in the other direction is of the cave trail heading toward the looming cliffs of Grotto Mountain and disappearing into a forest of lodgepole pine and Douglas fir on the flanks of the mountain. Once on the trail, one is unaware of the adjacent quarries, the distant cement plants, the rail and roads through the Bow Valley and the growing town of Canmore extending eastward down the valley. This piece of wilderness provides an increasingly important protective buffer for the cave, which urgently needs to be protected.

The setting is impressive and it is this, along with the fascination of the underground environment that we want to preserve for posterity. Visitors to Banff come for the high quality of this experience. Brent Richie, a professor in the Department of Environmental Design at the University of Calgary, offers us this about visitors for the coming years: "...we can expect travellers from countries with knowledge-based economies to be more experienced, more discerning and more demanding. In particular, we can expect that they will be seeking more individualized experiences often characterized as special interest travel." He goes on to suggest that rather than hands-off entertainment, visitors will prefer to enrich their lives with interactive, highly involved, quality travel experiences that focus on in-depth coverage of the special interest topic or destination at hand.

Names inscribed in moonmilk. Photo Dave Thomson.

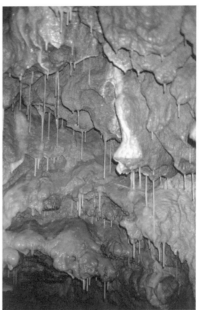

Stalactite before being removed by vandals.
Photo Dave Thomson.

The remnant of this stalactite.
Photo Dave Thomson.

This, we like to think, defines our cave tour experience almost completely. Further, we emphasize the personal touch of having only small groups. Indeed, a bond of friendship is built up during the tour that often extends to a place of refreshment afterward and continuing correspondence. The wild cave tour challenges our visitors both physically and mentally—and the challenge isn't always in one direction, as the guides will testify!

The cave certainly meets the criteria of "special interest travel" in that it is a unique activity in the region. Moreover, increasing numbers of the four or more million people that visit Banff National Park are looking for just this kind of hands-on experience. The hotel travellers have changed complexion in the last decade: less and less view the mountains from rented cars and tour buses, more are seeking the kind of experience that ecotourism offers. The numbers of ecotourists, particularly those looking for one-day experiences, are currently doubling every three years in western Canada. Other parts of the world are seeing a similar increase.

Our wild cave tour grew out of giving courses on cave science assisted by funding from the Science Alberta Foundation. The foundation's mandate is to transmit science to the general public via an interesting medium. We proposed that caves, or Rat's Nest Cave in particular, would be an interesting vehicle for science. My research over the years at the cave, along with some other studies, meant that we could give an informed if somewhat speculative interpretation of the natural history of the site. As full-time guides, Jon Rollins and I bring appropriate skills to the interpretive experience; we are both graduates in cave science as well as being active cavers. We have other part-time and occasional guides: Warwick Baggs, Bari Barabas, Maria Cashin, Mark Crapelle, Randy Spahl Troy Arnold and Dave Thomson, all of whom have been caving for years and have the relevant academic background (geography, geology and so on). We all have experience in cave rescue and first aid and are members of the provincial caving group, the Alberta Speleological Society. Between us we can account for well over 100 years of caving in many parts of the world!

None of this would have been possible without cooperation from the quarry company that holds a lease over the cave entrance: Continental Lime Limited (now Graymont Western Canada Inc.), based out of Calgary, but whose head office is in Utah. Their concerns, as conveyed to us, are of liability because they operate a large limestone quarry on Grotto Mountain about 1.5 km from the cave entrance, and blast the rock there several times a year. A consultant from California, who operates three tourist caves and has knowledge of industrial operations near caves, was able to allay fears that blasting could cause rock fall and injure tourists. In fact, I have been in the cave when blasting has been in progress, and the cave rings faintly but solidly in a bell-like tone. It's actually a rather safe place to be and, in the section on minerals, you'll see that even the most fragile deposits are unaffected by blasting. There could, however, be some risk from falling debris to individuals out on the mountainside, although no incident has occurred in 10 years of guiding at the cave. Despite success in running our operation, our relationship with Continental has not been easy. The management road continues to be long and rocky, but our relations currently are excellent.

Aside from liability, let's face it: active quarrying and tourism do not mix. They're industries essentially at loggerheads, which often have opposing goals. Indeed, the main reason for the Californian consultant coming (he was commissioned by the province—Travel Alberta), was to assess the tourism potential of the cave—something my company would be very interested in. He predicted that with lighting, trails and stairways, around a quarter of a million people would want to visit the cave annually. It is hard for us not to be attracted, although we envisage (and have subsequently recommended) far less numbers of people on a wilder type of tour; a tour that does not impact the ecological integrity of the cave and its surroundings.

We lobbied to get the cave designated as a Provincial Historic Site in the hope of acquiring a recreational lease to the cave and having some say (as speleologists) in the destiny of the cave. It's worth mentioning at this point that the entrance is a mere 34 m into the quarry lease, and 90 per cent of the known cave lies outside the lease. The historic designation came in March, 1987. It protects a square mile area around the entrance, but the custodianship still falls on the leaseholder, Continental Lime Limited. Up to the time of writing, we had been given permission to guide at the cave, under an agreement between Continental and Alberta Community Development (Alberta Culture). In fact, any bona fide groups or individuals could apply to these two interested parties for access, but it was very difficult, cumbersome and took time. Now, the management of the site has been granted to our company, which greatly streamlines the access process. In any event, with our extensive guiding experience we are probably in a better position to vet groups who want to visit the cave.

Various sensitive areas in the Bow corridor amounting to 46,000 acres have recently been protected. The Environment minister, Ty Lund, praised the efforts of various local groups who put in an enormous amount of volunteer time. One of the many positive outcomes has been the creation of the new Bow Valley Wildland Park; a result of successful lobbying by the "Special Places 2000 Program Local Coordinating Committee." The idea to have pro-tected lands in the Bow Valley was conceptualized by a local resident, Gareth Thompson, along with the Canadian Parks and Wilderness Society (CPAWS) and the Bow Valley Naturalists (BVN).

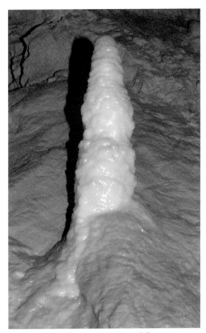

Stalagmite in the tour section of the cave. Photo Dave Thomson.

However, Grotto Mountain has not been included, which also means exclusion of the cave despite its historic status. The rock industry, which comprises a number of com-panies in the valley, insists it could not survive if this so-called Northeast Sector restricted their exploiting the area for future quarrying. The scar created by the removal of limestone from Grotto Mountain has created one of the largest visual impacts in the Bow Valley. Despite the extensive quarrying, recreation and some private development go apace on the mountain. This includes rock climbing, hiking, bighorn sheep bow hunting, horse riding, nature walks, a bed-and-breakfast and ranch, and of course caving. With the rapid development of Canmore as a resort

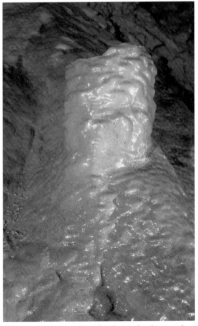

The same stalagmite after being broken and removed by vandals. Photo Dave Thomson.

destination, some feel the entire mountain corridor from Banff National Park eastward should be appropriately managed as a tourist region. In any event, Thompson urges education and enforcement if the existing special places are to be more than "paper parks." The historic designation for Rat's Nest Cave could be viewed likewise if strong management strategies are not implemented.

One hears a great deal about the "carrying capacity" of delicate areas, of which the cave is considered a special case. Tom Aley, director of the Ozark Underground Laboratory in the USA (a good model for us), has pointed out the carrying capacity of a cave is actually zero. One person going into a pristine cave will impact it, leave footprints, finger marks and so on, which irreversibly changes the cave ecology. The mechanisms that exist for self-healing in the surface environment are absent underground.

Now complementary management concepts are being applied: the Recreational Opportunity Spectrum (ROS) and the Limits of Acceptable Change (LAC). The first requires that caves, or various parts of caves, be classified in terms of their potential uses, likely impacts and resulting environmental conditions. This could mean that parts of caves might be suitable for heavy traffic (perhaps the tour routes that impact 10 per cent of the known cave), whereas other sensitive areas (the Pearly Way) would be off limits. The second concept, Limits of Acceptable Change, is concerned with defining those environmental conditions with the aim of maintaining them. Thus monitoring the cave environment (such as we do) becomes important where one might look at the preservation of cave formations, the changes in climate variables such as carbon dioxide, humidity, temperature, affects on bat roosts and other key indicators (or Valued Ecosystem Components—VEC). For example, humidity changes in the cave atmosphere can result in the drying out of cave formations and can also affect the cave-adapted fauna. A very severe impact at the popular Cadomin Cave to the north of us is people entering the cave during winter when the bats are hibernating. If these bats are woken up, they use critical amounts of body fat as they emerge from their torpid state and do not have enough stored fat to see them through the hibernating period. Signs ask people not to enter the cave from October to April. A valuable tool at Cadomin has been a register at the entrance from which numbers of visitors can be estimated—currently around 2000 per year.

The ROS, LAC and VEC concepts can be combined into Visitor Impact Management (VIM), where management goals are sought having identified key indicators for monitoring. The goals would normally include defining desired limits for the key indicators, monitoring those indicators and establishing management responses to the monitoring results.

For Rat's Nest Cave, some key indicators are the disturbance to mineral formations, cave surfaces, cave sediments, water bodies and biota (see pages 128 and 129). Mineral formations have been broken and removed or handled by muddy gloves. We have had some success in cleaning formations, but unfortunately mud tends to be cemented into the deposit as the formation grows. Cave surfaces have been vandalized and graffiti is a problem. If

Removing finely-layered mud samples for paleomagnetic analysis. Photo Dave Thomson.

removed quickly, the graffiti does not build up. The breakage of delicate wall features such as fluting is a problem, but it is probably the tracking of muddy sediments along the floor that has the greatest visual impact. One way to prevent this is to limit passage through the cave along clearly defined trails and to tape off delicate areas. The Wedding Cake Passage has been severely impacted by trail overwidening such that fragile rimstone dams have been trampled. Polishing of the rock surfaces owing to boots and cave suits has removed some delicate wall features especially around the entrance.

Ropes polish and cut grooves at the head of pitches. Water bodies are affected by sediment tracking and lose their clarity. The water in the cave is usually ponded and is static or slow-moving at best. The mineral-saturated water lines the pools with formations known as coralloids, and in their natural state these pools are crystal-clear. Mud tracked into the pools settles on the coralloids and severely limits the clarity of the pools. The affect on biota, mainly fauna, is very hard to estimate. However, the larger beasts—wood rats and bats—do not seem to have been significantly affected over the years by human use. In the case of the bats, we think it is because they roost in an undiscovered part of the cave. Should we one day find that place, we will almost certainly place it off limits, especially during winter hibernation. The wood rats appear to be habituated to us. Perhaps over the years they have learned we are not predators and need not fear us. In fact, our occasionally discarded items provide a useful supply of nesting material! Over-wintering bugs such as the harvestmen (daddy long-legs) seem to be little affected by visitors as they occupy out-of-the-way nooks and crannies within the cave.

At present only a couple of studies have been undertaken at the cave by us (a baseline study followed by a management study—see the further reading list), but more work urgently needs to be done so that appropriate management strategies can be put into place. Currently, the cave can be found on the recreational maps to the area, and the population of Alberta, especially Calgary, is increasing rapidly. The pressure for using the cave recreationally is increasing proportionally. In fact, all outdoor activities are experiencing increased participation. One mode for control is to conduct tours as we do. In restricting ourselves to guiding in a small section of the cave (less than 10 per cent of the entire known system), the remaining portion of the cave is not impacted except by experienced cavers or speleologists. Furthermore, we monitor our activities to make sure impacts are minimized and are acceptable within the definition of limits of acceptable change.

For protection and conservation, the cave has been gated by Continental Lime, but gating itself has impacts. It can alter the airflow in a cave and change the meteorology and, if not properly designed, can bar access to fauna—pack rats and bats in this case. Gates are also unsightly and detract from the wilderness experience. The gate at Rat's Nest Cave is designed so bats can easily fly between the bars, which also means that wood rats have no difficulty in getting in and out of the cave.

The gate is hated by some people who feel it is their right to have unimpeded access to the cave. To some extent I can sympathize with them, especially if they have been visiting the cave for many years. In the past simply keeping cave entrances secret was an effective management strategy and it wasn't necessary to block the cave because only a few well-informed people were visiting it. However, now that the cave is well known, we have seen the gates vandalized, graffiti appearing on the walls, cave formations broken and/or removed, the Bone Bed disturbed so that it is not such an attractive study site, many skulls taken and so on. The damage is actually not too severe thus far, but without management we could lose the site to posterity. As an example of effective cave management, the Alberta Speleological Society volunteering at Cadomin Cave have been cleaning up garbage, removing spray paint off the walls and generally educating the public about caves through appropriate signage. They are setting a splendid example especially as some of them are operating from Edmonton more than 300 km away. Through these efforts the cave has become somewhat self-policing, but problems do remain.

A similar initiative at Rat's Nest Cave is now being undertaken and we hope to see other fine accessible cave sites in the Canadian Rocky Mountains receive a similar level of involvement by interested groups. Recalling a T-shirt that said, "bats need friends," well, so do caves!

One vision for the cave is to construct an interpretive centre. This could be placed on the benches about 1.5 km from the cave, or in Canmore. Providing a focus, the interpretive centre could not only cater to visitors, but to cave specialists coming from all quarters of the world. Tourism could help in supporting these activities. The Karst Research Institute in

Postojna, Slovenia, the Karst Waters Institute in West Virginia and the Cave Works in Western Australia serve as fine examples of what can be done. An alternative approach is that of setting up a foundation, which could be backed by sponsorship and tourist revenues. A good example locally is the world famous Burgess Shale in nearby Field, British Columbia.

The increased knowledge of the cave by other people, aside from the considerable research benefits, would ensure fresh perspectives maintaining the enthusiasm of the guides and providing a site interpretation both stimulating and exciting to visitors. Hopefully, many educational institutions would be involved strengthening their programs in unique ways. Some years ago, I wrote a paper in the international journal *Cave and Karst Science* entitled "Studies at Rat's Nest Cave: Potential for an Underground Laboratory in the Canadian Rocky Mountains," in which I envisaged a number of programs at the cave. These comprise: Quaternary studies of speleothems including the regional glacial history, paleontological inventory of the Bone Bed, climate studies on speleothems, monitoring of the cave climate, macro- and micro-faunal studies, cave hydrology including sediments, cave exploration and finally educational programs. Currently, two students, Heidi Macklin (University of Calgary) and Feride Serefidin (McMaster University), are working at the cave studying the speleobiology and geology (age dating) respectively.

Thus in future years when you visit the cave you may find yourself hiking up onto the benchlands below the cave to an interpretive centre with magnificent views of the Bow Valley. The intention would be to develop the cave environs keeping in mind its sense of wildness and its ecological integrity.

Carrot formation. Photo Dave Thomson.

AREAS OF CONCERN UNDERGROUND

Underground Karst Components	• Potential Areas of Concern
Sediments, clastic material and bedrock features (speleogens)	•Removal of cave passage, increase in sedimentation from quarrying activities •Sediment compacting from passage of persons •Sediment and clastic material disturbance/redistribution (mud) from passage of persons •Bedrock erosion (especially near drops) damage to delicate box-work and polishing from foot traffic •Bedrock damage owing to rigging ropes/ladders and associated anchors
Mineral deposits (speleothems)	•Removal through destruction of cave passages from quarrying activities •Breakage and removal (inadvertent and vandalism) •Discolouration and disfigurement (touching, mud distribution, particulates) •Growth disruption through alteration to cave climate (see below)
Features of archaeological and paleontological interest	•Removal through destruction of cave passages from quarrying activities •Disturbance (mixing of stratified material, trampling and compacting) •Removal of bones
Fauna	•Dislocation and disturbance through destruction of cave passages from quarrying activities •Harassment or disturbance to pack rats, bats, harvesters and other as yet unidentified cave dwellers by caving activities •Disturbance to nesting/roosting sites by caving activities •Alteration to cave climate (see below) •Degradation of water quality for aquatic invertebrates (see below)
Air and Water Quality	•Interruption and sedimentation of subsurface drainage channels, pollution from fuel spills and explosive residues from quarrying activities •Alteration to cave environment parameters, i.e., relative humidity, temperature, CO_2 particulate matter through large numbers of persons entering cave •Pollution of water with sewage or chemicals such as carbide waste from caving activities •Increased turbidity of water from caving activities

By Jon Rollins, 1999

VALUED ECOSYSTEM COMPONENTS UNDERGROUND

Key Environmental Component or Resource	Valued Ecosystem Component (VEC) (Key Indicators)
Speleothems	•Calcite flowstone, rimstone, stalactites, stalagmites, columns, moonmilk, helictites, spar, coatings and crusts, subaqueous coralloids •Sediment deposits
Speleogens	•Bedrock passage floors, walls and ceilings •Scallops, box work
Air Quality and Flow	•Temperature •CO_2 levels •Relative humidity •Particulate matter •Direction and flow rate
Water Quality and Flow	•Chemistry •Turbidity •Pathogens
Fauna	•Wood rats •Bats •Harvesters

By Jon Rollins, 1999

Group of cavers in the Grand Gallery. Photo Ian Drummond.

Glossary

Active Carrying water.

Age (of cave) Radiometric methods have been used in the cave to date mineral deposits (Uranium-Thorium and carbon-14 methods). The cave starts life completely filled with water and passages enlarge with time owing to the acid effect of that water. Later through uplift or external valley deepening the cave may drain thus allowing mineral drip stones (speleothems) to form. Therefore, the "age" is actually a minimum age for the cave as there can be a substantial period between the water passage-forming period and subsequent mineral formation.

Amphipod Several species of troglobitic (cave-limited) crustaceans (amphipods). They are commonly found in tropical caves.

Anastomosis The development of a network of branching, intersecting and rejoining channels in a two-dimensional system. Anastomosing tubes, or cave anastomoses, which are generally formed owing to dissolution by slow, poorly directed, phreatic flow along a bedding-plane or fracture in limestone (or between a limestone surface, such as a passage ceiling, and in-washed sediments), represents an important element in the early stages of cave development. Individual anastomoses most commonly have a diameter of around 100 mm and networks may contain hundreds of tubes. Most anastomoses are abandoned when one channel offers preferential flow conditions so that it increases in size at the expense of others.

Anhydrite A calcium sulphate mineral like gypsum, but which does not contain water of crystallization. Gypsum strata lose their water of crystallization to form anhydrite when deeply buried.

Antecedent drainage In the case of the Rockies, represents valleys, which were down-cut as the mountains rose during the mountain-building phase.

Aragonite A pseudomorph of calcite ($CaCO_3$).

Ascenders Ratchet devices such as Jumars, which allow one to climb ropes.

Aven Also domepit. A hole in the roof of a cave passage that may be either a rather large blind roof pocket or a tributary inlet into the cave system.

Bedding plane A primary depositional lamination in sedimentary rocks. The plane is commonly exploited by groundwater in carbonate rocks and is thus a focal point for cave development.

Benches Glacial-alluvial terraces at the side of U-shaped glacial valleys. In the vicinity of Rat's Nest Cave these are as a result of an ancient lake dammed up by glacial ice.

Bicarbonate Calcite ($CaCO_3$) when dissolved in water (H_2O) forms Ca^{++} calcium ions and HCO_3^- bicarbonate ions. Bicarbonate ions are the source of hard water.

Brachiopod Similar to a clam except the opposing shells were of different sizes, the lower larger shell being attached by a "foot" to the sea floor.

Brachiopods can be found in the cave bearing rock at Rat's Nest Cave (circa 340 million years old).

Breaching Cave systems can be breached by external agents such as glaciers or surface streams. At Rat's Nest Cave entrance, breaching was caused by meltwater entrained under a rotting ice sheet as the glaciers retreated.

Breakdown Large pieces of bedrock that have collapsed from the ceiling of the cave passage, sometimes forming a Breakdown Chamber.

Bryozoan An early coral-like organism. Bryozoans can be found in the cave bearing rock at Rat's Nest Cave (circa 340 million years old).

Calcite A transparent mineral in the spar form, which often looks white in caves. Also calcium carbonate ($CaCO_3$), which constitutes the majority of cave minerals.

Calcium sulphate Also gypsum ($CaSO_4.2H_2O$) and anhydrite ($CaSO_4$).

Cambrian The Cambrian period lasted from 544-510 million years. It is significant in the Canadian Rockies because of its association with the Burgess Shale.

Carbonic acid Forms when carbon dioxide is dissolved in water as H_2CO_3. It is an important agent in karst processes as it dissolves limestone and dolomite to form caves.

Carboniferous The Carboniferous period lasted from 353-300 million years. In North America this period is broken up into the earlier Mississippian and later Pennsylvanian. The cave is formed in Mississippian limestone.

Cave radio A radio working on long-wavelength (low frequency) radio waves that can transmit through bedrock.

Chert A silicious mineral derived from sponges and other marine-like organisms, which can be found in limestone and dolomite. Chert can be found in Rat's Nest Cave, where, owing to its insolubility in groundwater, it projects from the cave walls as flags. The early aborigines used chert for stone tools.

Chimney wind In winter the cave interior is warmer than outside, therefore warm air rises out of higher entrances. In summer the opposite is the case; relatively cool interior air drains out of lower entrances. Rat's Nest Cave has one entrance where the higher part of the entrance acts as an upper opening, and the lower portion acts as a lower opening. Such air flows are called chimney winds.

Choke When a cave entrance or passage is impenetrably blocked with boulders or sediment, it is said to be choked. Caves are often extended by digging through chokes.

Clastic Siliceous material produced by the weathering of other rocks, often transported and deposited in caves by water.

Clinometer A survey device that measures inclinations between survey stations.

Coatings and Crusts See Chapter 7 for definition.

Column A stalagmite growing up to meet a downward growing stalactite.

Conulite See Chapter 7 for definition.

Coralloid See Chapter 7 for definition.

Corrasion Also called mechanical erosion, it occurs as water-borne sediment wears away the cave surfaces.

Cretaceous The Cretaceous period lasted from 144-65 million years, known for the dinosaur extinction at its end. It is associated with the coal measures in the Canmore area.

Crinoid Crinoids are echinoderms, in the same group that includes starfish. They live today as "sea lilies," although they are animals, not plants. Crinoids evolved in the Cambrian but were not common in the Rockies until the Mississippian, when they were common. They can be seen in the bedrock in Rat's Nest Cave.

Curtain See Chapter 7 for definition.

Dating See age of cave.

Devonian The Devonian period lasted from 410-353 million years. Devonian rocks can be seen on the walk up to the cave on the other side of the valley.

Dip Dip and "strike" are terms used to describe the location of cave passages in relation to the bedding structure of the rock in which they are contained.

Dip tube A phreatic cave passage running down dip.

Dissolution The process by which rock is chemically dissolved by acid groundwater.

Doline A circular closed depression. Dolines may form by dissolution and/or collapse from below. These are absent at Rat's Nest, but are common in limestone alpine areas such as the Ptolemy Plateau in the Crowsnest Pass.

Dolomite The pure mineral dolomite has the composition $CaMg(CO_3)_2$ and has properties similar to calcite. The rock dolomite consists mainly of the dolomite mineral with some calcite, and has properties very similar to limestone. The natural dissolution of dolomite is generally slower than limestone. Hence dolomite karst is less well developed than limestone karst, although extensive cave systems do exist in dolomite. Dolomite is extensive in the Front and Main ranges of the Rockies. Its composition grades form dolomite to limestone, hence dolomitic limestone regularly occurs. The Rat's Nest Cave bearing limestone is, however, rather pure, as is the limestone nearby in the quarry.

Domepit See aven.

Drapery See curtain.

Duck A short section of flooded passage, with sufficient airspace to breathe.

Dye tracing The use of concentrated dye, usually rhodamine or fluorocene, to discover drainage routes taken by subterranean streams.

Ecological integrity Refers to the cave environment in a holistic sense and is an important concept for cave management.

Ecotourism An active style of tourism, which has low impacts and whose aim is sustainability. At Rat's Nest the tour offers both an adventurous experience and a strong natural history interpretation by informed guides.

Entrenchment See vadose.

Eocene The Eocene epoch lasted from 56.5-34 million years.

Etriers Short, stirrup-like ladders used in artificial climbing.

Evaporite A rock such as gypsum or rock salt (halite) formed from evaporating lagoons.

Fault A fracture in the Earth's crust, across which relative rock movement has taken place, or continues to take place. Fault planes commonly guide vertical or sub-vertical shafts in caves as well as guiding sub-horizontal (common in the Rockies) or oblique passages within the confines of the fault plane.

Flowstone See Chapter 7 for definition.

Formations Also speleothems or mineral formations.

Fossil Opposite of active, a fossil cave or cave passage no longer carrying water.

Fracture A break or secondary discontinuity in the rock mass, whether or not there has been relative movement across it. Faults, thrusts and joints are all fractures, but bedding-planes, which are primary features, are not.

Geothermal heating Heating of rocks and groundwater from the Earth's interior. Rockies' caves are generally at a higher temperature than the mean annual temperature at the surface owing to geothermal heating.

Glacial refugium Refers to caves underling glacial regions often containing microfauna (e.g., amphipods), which, protected by the cave, can survive glacial periods.

Groundwater In general use this is subsurface water, whether above or below the water table. Strictly, however, groundwater refers only to water that lies below the water table, in the saturated or phreatic zone.

Helictite See Chapter 7 for definition.

Hibernaculum In the cave context, a chamber or passage, where bats hibernate.

Holocene See Quaternary.

Hydraulic gradient See water table.

Hydrology The movement of water underground. The subterranean drainage systems provided by caves are very ancient, and often bare no relationship to surface drainage basins.

Hypsithermal An unusually warm period during the holocene.

Ice-contact cave A cave formed by basal glacial meltwater at a point where glacial ice is in direct contact with the bedrock. Many caves in the Rockies appear to have, or have had, an intimate association with glaciers.

Ice-free corridor The ice-free region that was present during the major glaciations when the Rocky Mountain ice sheets failed to meet the continental ice sheet extending from the east. The corridor is significant in that it allowed humans from Asia to penetrate southward into North America.

Inception horizons Part of a rock succession that is particularly susceptible to the effects of the earliest cave-forming processes and hence is critical to the origin of most caves. By virtue of physical, lithological or chemical deviation from the predominate carbonate strata within the sequence, it passively or actively favours the localized inception (or initiation) of dissolutional activity.

Interglacial The period between the ice ages.

Joint A tectonic fracture that has not suffered any relative movement as in a fault. Joints in limestone or dolomite favour the formation of limestone pavements, good examples of which are seen in glaciated alpine areas in the Rockies. Joints also can direct cave passage formation.

Jurassic Preceding the Cretaceous period, the Jurassic period lasted from 206-144 million years.

Juvenile Karst in which the subterranean drainage routes have not been enlarged enough to produce enterable cave passages.

Karren Collective name for a variety of small solution grooves and other such features found on bedrock surfaces in karst areas.

Karst A landscape created on soluble rock with efficient underground drainage. Karst is characterized by caves, dolines, a lack of surface drainage and other climatically controlled features, and is mainly, but not exclusively, formed on limestone. The name derives from the German form of Kras—the classical karst straddling the border between Slovenia and Italy. In the modern context karst is being conceptualized as a suite of processes involving groundwater and soluble rocks.

Keyhole passage One that contains an upper phreatic portion (tube), which has subsequently been entrenched by vadose streams to form a lower canyon portion. Castleguard Cave, for example, contains many kilometres of such passages, whereas Rat's Nest Cave contains almost none.

Limestone Sedimentary rock containing at least 50% calcium carbonate by weight. The purer limestones (e.g., at Rat's Nest Cave) consist almost entirely of calcite; less pure rock may be referred to as muddy limestones, for example. Some limestones are porous with diffuse permeability; these rarely become truly cavernous, though some fissure flow may occur. Where groundwater flow in less porous rocks is restricted to bedding related fissures and secondary fractures it can, even when moving very slowly, corrode the almost entirely soluble rock and lead to true cave development.

Mechanical erosion See corrasion.

Montane Refers here to the typical plant communities that cover the lower slopes and foothills of the Rockies. The Bow Valley, over which Rat's Nest Cave looks, is a typical montane region.

Moonmilk See Chapter 7 for definition.

Overburden Refers to the thickness of rock overlying caves.

Paleoenvironment In the context of caves, refers to the past conditions in the cave and on the surface above the cave.

Paleohydrology The past condition of water flow in the cave. In Rat's Nest Cave, solution features of the walls and ceiling give information concerning flow rates of glacial meltwater in the past.

Paleontology Study of fossils.

Paleozoic The Paleozoic era extended from the Cambrian to the Permian periods (544-250 million years).

Paragenesis A type of cave passage development in which erosion of the passage floor is inhibited by an armouring layer of sediment, such that any dissolutional enlargement is dominantly upward. Pendants and anastomosing channels can result at the ceiling when the armouring sediment completely fills the passage.

Permafrost A perennially frozen zone in the subsurface. Some ice caves (rock caves that contain permanent ice) in the Rockies, especially in the Crowsnest Pass, are contained within permafrost zones.

Permian The Permian period extended from 300-250 million years.

Phreatic zone or phreas The zone of saturated rock below the water table, within which all conduits and subconduits are water filled (sometimes referred to as the flooded, phreatic or saturated zone). Commonly the phreatic zone is considered as being subdivided into an upper (shallow phreatic) zone, middle (deep phreatic or bathyphreatic) zone and a lower stagnant phreatic zone.

Pitch Vertical section of cave passage requiring a rope to descend or ascend.

Pleistocene See Quaternary.

Pseudomorph A mineral that takes on an unusual crystal shape (habit) similar to another mineral of different composition.

Quaternary The Quaternary period, 1.65 million years to the present day, comprises the Pleistocene epoch (1.65-0.01 million years) and the Holocene (the last 10,000 years). The Pleistocene comprises all of the major glaciations, whereas the Holocene encompasses the period after the last major (Wisconsin) glaciation.

Raft See Chapter 7 for definition.

Rappel A method of descend down ropes using a friction device.

Resurgence A spring, which may be an enterable cave, where water flows out to the surface. Such caves often may be accessed only by diving.

Rift passage A fault or joint guided cave passage, usually tall and narrow in cross-section.

Rigging The use of ropes and attachment points (pitons, bolts, chocks) to progress through a vertical cave system.

Rimstone dams See Chapter 7 for definition.

Scallop A spoon-shaped carving in a cave wall, floor or ceiling owing to solutional erosion by eddies in flowing water. The direction and velocity of the flowing water can be determined from their asymmetry and size (usually from 1 cm to 1 m in length).

Sinkholes (Sinks) Points at which water goes underground (recharge), common in karst areas (see dolines).

Siphon Synonym for sump, refers to a section of flooded cave passage.

Soda straws Tubular stalactites. See Chapter 7 under stalactites.

Spar See Chapter 7 for definition.

Speleobiology The study of cave life (flora, fauna and fungi).

Speleogenesis Although the term literally means the birth, origin or mode of formation of caves, the full extent of speleogenesis includes all of the changes that take place between the inception (initiation) and the eventual destruction of an underground drainage system. It includes development phases during which the active drainage voids are too small to be considered caves, as well as phases when the cave no longer functions as a drain, is enlarged only by collapse and, eventually, is being totally removed.

Speleogenic Conducive to cave formation.

Speleogens The counterpart to speleothems, these are features carved out of passage surfaces such as scallops and solution pockets.

Speleology Scientific study of caves, including aspects of science such as geomorphology, geology, hydrology, chemistry, physics and biology, and also the many techniques of cave exploration.

Speleothem General term for all cave mineral deposits (see Chapter 7). Most are forms of calcite whose precipitation processes, related mainly to carbon dioxide levels in the water, are the direct reverse of the dissolution of limestone.

Stalactite See Chapter 7 for definition.

Stalagmite See Chapter 7 for definition.

Strike See dip.

Sulphide minerals Minerals that are composed of one or more metals combined with sulphur. The most common is pyrite. They are believed to be produced by the metabolic action of microorganisms. Sulphides can be oxidized during speleogenesis to form sulphuric acid, which aids in the cave forming processes.

Sulphur-reducing bacteria Bacteria living close to the surface of deep springs that can reduce sulphate to hydrogen sulphide.

Sump Also siphon. When a cave passage encounters the water table, or more commonly a U-shaped section of passage filled with water, it is said to sump. Sumps generally require diving equipment to pass through unless very short.

Thread A hole in the rock-wall of a cave passage that provides a natural attachment point for ropes (see rigging).

Thrust fault See fault.

Thrutch A caver's colloquial term used to describe moving with difficulty along a narrow passage.

Tricounis Three-pointed cleats embedded in the soles of boots used at the turn of the century for mountaineering.

Troglobites Life forms that live permanently in the dark-zone, and are found exclusively in caves.

Troglophiles Life forms that may complete their entire life cycle in caves, but species of the same type are found on the surface.

Trogloxenes Life forms that visit caves, sometimes for hibernation purposes.

Tubular Stalactites See soda straws.

Underfit stream One that is running in an oversized channel caused by higher flows in the past.

U-shaped valley A valley scoured out by glaciers.

Vadose zone The zone of rock above the water table, containing a dominant proportion of cavities with free downward drainage that is only partially water-filled. The vadose zone is also referred to as the unsaturated zone, and is commonly accepted to comprise (in descending order) the soil, a subcutaneous or epikarstic zone, and a free-draining percolation zone.

Varve Very fine sedimentary layers are deposited in placid, stationary water.

Vibrissae More commonly, whiskers. These are very well developed on bushy-tailed wood rats that need to find their way through dark caves.

Water table The top surface of a body of slowly moving groundwater that fills the pore spaces within a rock mass. Above it lies the freely draining vadose zone, and below it lies the permanently saturated phreas. The water table slope (hydraulic gradient) is low in limestone owing to the high permeability, and the level controlled by outlet springs or local geological features. High flows create steep hydraulic gradients and hence rise in the water level away from the spring. Local water tables in caves can vary by as much as 450 m!

Caving Organizations in Western Canada

Some of the general objectives of caving groups in Canada are: locate, explore, survey and record caves; to conserve the caves for future generations to appreciate; to promote safe caving practices; to advance the understanding and appreciation of caves; cave conservation. For anyone wanting to know more about Canadian caving, the most useful source of information can be found on Caving Canada: www.cancaver.ca/, the Canadian Cave and Karst information server. Another excellent source of information is the national caving magazine the *Canadian Caver*, which has been published for more than 30 years. It is produced semi-annually for and by Canadian cavers, providing accounts of caving expeditions, publishing surveys of cave systems in Canada and elsewhere and a variety of other cave-related articles of interest to cavers.

British Columbia

British Columbia Speleological Federation (BCFS): The BCSF is the central organization for caving in British Columbia, coordinating the efforts of many in the fields of conservation, safety, rescue, exploration, education and technical expertise. Constituent groups consist of the Chilliwack River Valley Cavers, Golden Speleological Society, Prince George Devil's Club, Vancouver Island Cave Exploration Group, University of Northern B.C. Caving Club, University of Victoria Caving Club, Vancouver Caving Group and Under Achievers Caving Group. They publish *BC Caver* four times per year.

Vancouver Island Cave Exploration Group (VICEG): The group's organized caving began in 1962 as the B.C. Cave Hunters, and evolved into the Vancouver Island Cave Exploration Group in 1970. It has operated continuously as the main organized caving group since, both on Vancouver Island and mainland British Columbia. The club maintains good working relationships with the provincial parks branch, federal parks and the area's logging companies informing them of caves in their future working areas. With approximately 75 members, most of which are on the island, there are trips most weekends to various parts of the island.

Northwest Caving Association (NCA): The NCA is an organization made up of representatives from NSS Grottos (U.S. state speleological groups) in the northwest. The purpose of the NCA is to promote conservation, safety and communication among cavers in the northwestern United States and western Canada. Contact www.caves.org/region/nca/.

University of Victoria Caving Club: This club was established in 1974. It meets on the first and third Tuesday of every month, and is sponsored by the University of Victoria Sports and Recreation Department. Trips are made to various caves on Vancouver Island. The caves visited can be very demanding, so good physical shape is a must. Vertical rope work and team skills are taught before anyone is taken underground and all efforts are given to make each trip as safe as possible. The trip leaders are members of the VICEG and the club is affiliated with both the BCSF and the VICEG.

Northern Vancouver Island Cave and Karst Explorations: This group primarily operates in the north of the island. The director, Michael Henwood, can be contacted at caves@island.net.

University of Northern British Columbia Caving Club (UNBC): The club consists of a group of Prince George cavers who cave primarily in karst regions within two hours' drive of the city. There are occasional expeditions farther afield. Some of the finest caves in Canada are found in northern B.C. UNBC is a constituent member of the BCSF. The club can be contacted at: University of Northern British Columbia Office of Communications, 3333 University Way, Prince George, British Columbia, Canada V2N 4Z9 and http://quarles.unbc.edu/keen/netcave.htm.

The Under Achievers Cave Exploration Group: Founded in 1997, the club is based out of Kelowna, B.C., and serves as the centre for organized caving in the central Okanagan area of British Columbia. The club is a charter member of the BCSF. Contact www.cancaver.ca/bc/ua/.

Golden Speleological Society: Contact www.cancaver.ca/docs/groups/.

Alberta

Alberta Speleological Society (ASS): This group is the recognized caving authority in the province of Alberta, dedicated to the exploration, study and conservation of caves in the Canadian Rockies. It has set the caving standard in Canada for the last 30 years. The ASS is a club open to anyone interested in sporting or scientific aspects of caves in the Rocky Mountains, and willing to visit them in a safe, environmentally friendly manner. The ASS promotes the conservation of physical and biological features, to prevent the pollution of the cave environment and foster an appreciation of the value of caves as a natural resource to the general public. The club has several informal connections with many caving organizations worldwide. The membership comprises about 100 cavers ranging from first time novices to seasoned veterans with international caving experience. The ASS is also the volunteer steward for Cadomin Cave in partnership with Alberta Environment Protection. Contact www.caving.ab.ca/.

Saskatchewan

Alberta Speleological Society (Saskatoon): The ASS extends its influence to Saskatchewan. Contact www.cancaver.ca/docs/groups/.

Manitoba

Speleological Society of Manitoba: Established in 1987, the society is involved in various karst conservation projects within the province of Manitoba. It publishes the *Manitoba Cave Atlas*, *Caves of the Manitoba Interlake* and *Bats of Manitoba*. For information related to caving in Manitoba, contact www.cancaver.ca/prov/man/.

Index

Index